Jacques Villon: Cubist work on paper in the collection of Jack Leissring

Jacques Villon, Portrait d'Artiste, Color Aquatint and Drypoint, 1955

Jacques Villon

Cubist Work on Paper
in the Collection
of
Jack Leissring

Jack Leissring

Leissring, John (Jack) Cother, 1935

Jacques Villon,
Cubist Work on Paper in the Collection of Jack Leissring
Includes Bibliographic References

Published, 2013
J. C. Leissring Fine Art Press
Santa Rosa, CA

ISBN: 978-0-9630085-0-3

1. Villon, Jacques, 1875-1963
2. Cubism--France--Exhibitions

Cover: Jacques Villon: "L'Effort," Watercolor and gouache on paper, Catalog page: 113

Use of This Catalogue:

The prints are presented in the order of their creation with French and English titles. Quotes from sources are transcribed as written. "G&P" comments are translations from the French.

All notes and marks appearing on the prints are transcribed as shown.

Dimensions are taken at the plate mark or image, in the case of lithographs or paintings; Height precedes width.

Where work has been displayed in a bibliographic catalog, the proper reference is given as an abbreviation on the leading (left) page; abbreviations are explained on page 129. G&P references, which include "Exhibitions" and "Bibliography," are taken directly from the G&P text.

Contents

Preface — 1

Biography — 2

Villon the Artist — 3

Cubism — 9

Catalog — 22

Sources — 126

Abbreviations and Referenced Catalogs — 129

Preface

Jacques Villon, Self-Portrait
1909

One of the 20th Century's most significant artists, Jacques Villon's greatest talents were expressed through the medium of print-making. Stanley Hayter and others have called Villon "the father of modern print-making." Jacques Villon, actually named Gaston Duchamp, was probably the most significant *peintre-graveur* of the twentieth century in France. He was less of a revolutionary innovator than his youngest brother, Marcel, and therefore, had less of an impact on younger artists. Though he was a painter of considerable gifts, his best and most characteristic work is found in his engravings and etchings.

The first Duchamp brother of the famous trio, Gaston (Jacques Villon), Raymond Duchamp-Villon and Marcel, was born in the Normandy province of France in 1875. His earliest study was law, but he turned to art in 1894 and took the pseudonym, Jacques Villon. His first lithographs were executed in 1895 when he met Toulouse-Lautrec who exerted a great influence upon Villon's earliest works. After military service in 1898, he established his studio in Montmartre where he worked until 1906.

In that year, he moved to the Paris suburb of Puteaux. This was accompanied by a change in his artistic view. In 1912 he organized the art movement called "the Section d'Or exhibition" which included works by Marcel Duchamp, his own, his brother Raymond, Gleizes, Gris, Leger, Lhote, Marcoussis and Metzinger. In the period 1913-14, he executed his "Cubist" drypoints. He spent the next four years in the military service returning to Puteaux in 1919. In that year, he adopted an abstract style, but the postwar period was not a good one for artists. To earn a living, he and other artists copied each other's works in a variety of mediums--Villon executed 45 aquatints of the works of Bonnard, Modigliani and others. He visited the United States in 1936, received many prizes and awards in the ensuing years: Paris World's Fair, Carnegie International First Prize, Grand Prize, Venice Biennale, 1956, Grand Prize, Brussels World's Fair, 1958.

He died at his studio in Puteaux in 1963[1]

Jacques Villon, Puteaux, 1962

Biography

Villon's Grandfather, Emile Nicolle, Gaston Duchamp, Etching, 1891

Gaston Duchamp, age 15

Born Gaston Duchamp in Damville, Normandy, on July 31, 1875 to Marie-Caroline-Lucie (Nicolle) and Justin-Isidore (Eugene, Eusebe) Duchamp. The family moved to Blainville, near Rouen (North) after the elder Duchamp purchased a notary practice there. Gaston's maternal grandfather, Emile-Frederic Nicolle, worked as a ship-broker and was an ardent copper engraver of mainly architectural forms. There were five siblings, Raymond, born 1876 (died 1918), Marcel, 1889-1968, Suzanne, 1889-1963, Yvonne, 1895, and Magdeleine, 1898. He was sixteen in 1891, when he taught himself the fundamentals of engraving by observing his grandfather, Emile Nicolle.

The boy's father urged him to study law and in 1894, he travelled to Paris to study at the University of Paris. Later in the year, he returned to Rouen, studying at the School of Beaux-Arts, coming under the influence of Toulouse-Lautrec and even sending drawings to local illustrated newspapers, the Rouen Artiste, and L'Etudiant.

With his father's reluctant permission, he returned to Paris to study art but only if he continued his law studies. He stayed with his brother Raymond who was a medical student. Possibly to appease his father, he adopted the surname of a beloved French poet, Francois Villon and the first name, "Jack." He contributed to Parisian newspapers using that name and later-on as Jacques Villon. Perhaps, it has been suggested, in deference to Francois Villon, he "idiosyncratically anglicized his last name, not turning the double "l" into the "y" sound usual in French, but giving it full force, Vil-lon...The "Jacques" came from the "grande sympathie" for Alphonse Daudet's novel *Jack* indeed he spelled it "Jack" at first and the name "Jack Villon" was signed to a few very early drawings."[1]

Villon served with the infantry for a year in 1897, and afterward, had drawings accepted by the publications, Le Rire (with Toulous-Lautrec) and Le Courrier Francais, to which he contributed weekly until 1910. He remained in Montmartre as a contributor to newspapers, as a designer of posters, learning then the technique of lithography necessary for printing posters. Edmond Sagot became his publisher in 1899 and in 1901 he exhibited his first prints at the Societe Nationale, receiving some critical praise. The entire issue (No 46) of Assiette au Beurre was illustrated by Villon under the title: "La Vie Facile."

In 1904, he became a member of Salon d'Autumne, but later resigned because of conflicts over Cubism. He studied painting at the Academy Julian that year, and did many engravings in the Belle Epoque style. He married Gabrielle Bouef. He traveled back to Rouen for a year, but returned to Paris, Puteaux, where he lived out his life.[2]

Villon the Artist

The first exhibition of the "Section d'Or," a title suggested by Villon, was at the Galerie La Boetie, in October of 1912. Also in 1912, a new journal, La Section d'Or appeared; the Maison Cubiste, an architectural display of Andre Mare and others, showed at Salon d'Automne.

Villon and Raymond and Marcel exhibited at the famed Armory Show in New York in 1913. Villon showed nine paintings, all of which were sold. The Armory Show, the "International Exhibition of Modern Art," was organized by the Association of American Painters and Sculptors, at the Armory of the New York National Guard's Sixty-ninth Regiment, at 26th Street and Lexington Avenue, from February 17-March 15, 1913. It was chiefly organized by John Sloan, Arthur B. Davies, and Walt Kuhn.[1,2]

Armory Show Announcement
1913

Marcel Duchamp first submitted Nude Descending a Staircase to appear in a Cubist show at the Salon des Indépendants in Paris, but jurist Albert Gleizes asked Duchamp's brothers to have him voluntarily withdraw the painting, or paint over the title that he had painted on the work and rename it something else. The hanging committee objected to the work on the grounds that it had "too much of a literary title", and that "a nude never descends the stairs-a nude reclines".

Of the incident Duchamp recalled, "I said nothing to my brothers. But I went immediately to the show and took my painting home in a taxi. It was really a turning point in my life, I can assure you. I saw that I would not be very much interested in groups after that."

He submitted the painting to the 1913 Armory Show in New York City located where Americans, accustomed to naturalistic art, were scandalized. Julian Street, an art critic for the New York Times wrote that the work resembled "an explosion in a shingle factory," and cartoonists satirized the piece. It spawned dozens of parodies in the years that followed.[3]

Villon's increasing interest in the theoretical aspects of painting and form, likely influenced by association with Metzinger and the others, became enforced by examination and inculcation of da Vinci's theory of pyramidal perception. He was never completely convinced by the academic approach to painting. He described his theoretical basis to Alexander Watt in 1962: "I have always been, fundamentally, a figurative painter. I follow nature, taking certain liberties, I will admit, but it has always been reality that I seek to express."[4]

Thus it may be that his natural way of seeing and drawing corresponded to theoretical and even mathematical ideas. When I examined closely the hatching of his first etching, at age 16, the triangular (pyramidal) forms, spoken of by

Gaston Duchamp, Portrait of His Father, Etching, 1891

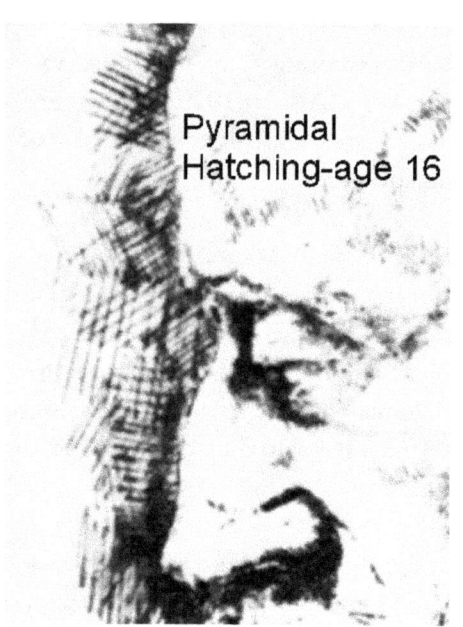

Gaston Duchamp, Age 16
Detail

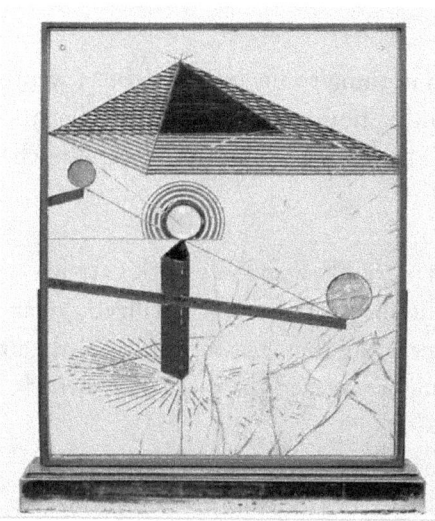

Marcel Duchamp, 1914-15

da Vinci, are already clear. To find that they corresponded to historical theories, the golden section (phi) and to Leonardo's theory of painting gave, perhaps, impetus to his focus upon formal fundamentals to support his own organizing theory of art. He articulates his philosophy in 1962, at the age of 87: "For me, the picture is a creation in which the subject—the pretext furnished by a perceived rhythm, expressive of our unconscious life brought to the level of consciousness—is translated into an area of color, into a hierarchy of colored planes. The whole is bound together by an arabesque, closely incorporated into the basic division of the canvas where all elements are brought into balance."[5]

Younger Marcel, in a reaction similar to that expressed above, made light of Villon's apparent obsession with formal ideas. In a punning title to a work emphasizing physical optical theory, (To Be Looked At, With One Eye, Close To, For Almost An Hour) he appears to chide his older brother.[5] From afar, for he completed this work in Argentina after he left France in 1914-15 (a prescient response to the horrors of the next four years in Europe). Duchamp's Egyptian pyramid in To Be Looked At... is a deliberate and mocking distortion of Leonardo's idea as it occurs, in the Treatise on Painting, at the center of his theory of optics.[6,7]

Duchamp made fun of the visual pyramid possibly because his brother Jacques Villon, was obsessed by it. Villon thought that Leonardo's pyramid and the golden section could provide theoretical support to make Cubism a classical art form. In 1915, the last time the two met until after the WWI, Villon was enthused by this idea. This theorizing began in 1911, when the brothers and their Cubist friends became fascinated by Leonardo's optical formulations: "This is the art of painting by pyramids," declared Leonardo, "for there is no object however small which is not larger than the point where these pyramids meet. Therefore, if you take the lines at the extremities of each body and if you can continue them to a certain point, then they will converge into the pyramidal form."[4]

And Villon asserts that by superimposing, on the painting, this pyramidal form, one obtains a density in which the interaction of echoing colors produces depth.

There is a theory in social psychology that personality traits among siblings are shared unequally, that what is taken by the eldest is no longer available to the younger, thus Jacques' formal reticence left a humorous trickster for Marcel, and intermediate traits for Raymond.[8]

Villon had long thought that there should be a way and a means of integrating the conception of the Cubists and of combining them with the scientific theories of the impressionists; hence the explanation of why Villon is sometimes called a Cubist-Impressionist painter.[4]

Marcel Duchamp discussed these ideas with his brother in the early days of Cubism. Then he chose a different path, a directly-perceptual method of creating transparency and overlapping planes in the visual field.[6]

Many of Villon's Cubist prints were gathered for an important exhibition in 2001 at the Philadelphia Museum of Art (PMA 2001). The prints included in the catalog range in dates from 1909 to 1951. The Philadelphia Museum publication includes Bal du Moulin Rouge (pages 39, 41, 43). The Cubist (style) prints in this collection are in the interval between 1909 and 1962.[9]

As we look more deeply into Villon's Cubist work, we will find that he, as so many artists, tended to revisit earlier problems and themes, extending, what some might hope to define as a distinct period, far into the full extent of his life and career as an artist. There is a tendency to divide an artist's working life into handy episodes. In a matter related to this, I was reminded of a conversation between artist Michael Ayrton (MA) and musician Yehudi Menuhin (YM), recorded at the BBC in 1973. Ayrton and Menuhin were discussing "originality" in art and music:

Giorgione, 1510

Michael Ayrton speaks first: "You see I think that there tends to be a deep misunderstanding about teaching of art and this may be true of music, but perhaps not. And, that is, that it should be original. Now if there is one thing that doesn't matter at all in the individual is whether he is original or not. It is rather like suggesting that when you sign a check it is your signature that matters, not what you have in the bank. Mimesis and imitation is the whole history of my art. Everyone imitated everybody available. But as luck would have it there wasn't so much available to imitate. Nonetheless one could make a catalog of seminal images, varying from the Greek through Giorgione's Dresden Venus to Titian's [Venus of Urbino] right up to Renoir and they would be copies of copies of copies, everyone making their own minute contribution, change, stylistically, the signature in the handwriting, but with the devout desire to imitate as clearly and as correctly as possible. This doesn't really exist in the arts, in my arts, anymore, because everybody is terrified that they are going to be accused of plagiarism, Well, it's quite unimportant."

Titian, 1538

YM: It's quite unimportant. The unfortunate thing is that mechanical reproduction, as you say, has flooded the world with imitations of every kind. And, to retain his identity, the artist wants to be recognized as somebody who is creative and therefore must create from nothing, which is impossible. "

MA: "It's a sad misconception, and its very very general, even in criticism, where anything that appears to be original however trivial will be extolled rather than something that is not overtly a novelty and which may be passed-over as dull. Perhaps it is irreversible, at least for the present time."[10]

All art is somehow infected by all other art. And, as the above conversation continues, Ayrton paraphrases W. H. Auden in saying that 'no man could become a complete human being without communication with the past.' The dialog that musicians and artists have with their own ancestry is perpetual and vital to their ability to make anything, whatever. Menuhin suggests that "we must be linked to what we are."[10]

The matter of starting from a completely blank canvas is in this way, impossible, for the linkage, the infection, so to speak, is permanent and, once begun, remains in the susceptible host--like the eukayrytic (with a nucleus) cell of the animal inheriting the mitochondria from bacterial or prokaryotic (without a nucleus) sources. Since Aristotle, it has been mankind's propensity to place things into categorical boxes. H.R. Arneson, in an essay in Art in America writes: "The problem of the verbal categorization of the visual arts will always exist. . .the question of whether a new direction is developing in American art is no sooner raised that the problem of what to call it is posed."[11]

Of course, it is not only "American" art. And, this name calling appears generally to begin with the critics. When Picasso and Braque were in the process of analyzing elements of classical painting they claimed that drawing had been more important in the history of painting than color. Drawing alone could fuse the various colors on the canvas into a picture. They invented a fundamental element of two black lines, which now formed the basis of all their paintings. The Parisian critic, Louis Vauxcelles, upon seeing a painting by Braque in 1908 described his work as "bizarre cubiques," reducing everything to "geometric schemes and cubes," thereby attaching for all time the interpretation to the artistic form. Clement Greenberg, in what many believe to be a great error, named the work of the action painters of New York: "Abstract Expressionism," whereas in fact the work was not an abstraction of anything, but was, rather, as pointed out by Lawrence Ferlinghetti (who grew-up in New York and painted there) : The so-called abstract expressionist work ". . . is a new creation, having no referent outside of itself."[13]

So it seems we are stuck with the term Cubism because we live in a world where humans have a preference for pat categories, for binary thinking, a world where people like to proffer narrow judgments: good, bad, expressionist, Cubist, Newtonian, quantum, pure, formal, jazz, classical and so on. For one significant reason, applying the word Cubist to a period of Villon's work is incorrect because the forms one might like to place into a "Cubist" pigeon hole are found in etchings, paintings and lithographs throughout his long ca-

"Monsieur Duchamp," Lithograph in color, 1962

reer. [see image at left]Thus, while Cubism was an era put to rest by historians and critics, the forms that these authorities assert as "Cubist" will be found in Villon's final work. The inclusion of transition work into this group of "Cubist" images intends to demonstrate the gradual flattening of the picture space, which, most authorities agree, is the essence of Braque's and Picasso's Cubist intent. The catalog thereby begins with several etchings completed in the years 1907-1909, and which have a distinctive "Belle-Epoque" reference, but which show the gradual loss of detail in the backgrounds of the dominant subject(s).

Is it even proper to classify Villon's work as "Cubist?" I wish to explore this in greater detail in the following essay.

1. Jacques Villon, Daniel Robbins, Ed., Fogg Art Museum, Harvard University, Cambridge, MA
2. http://www.acsu.buffalo.edu/~jconte/Armory_Show.html
3. http://en.wikipedia.org/wiki/Nude_Descending_a_Staircase,_No._2
4. Alexander Watt, Art in America, Vol 50, No,. 3, Fall, 1962, Page 115
5. Marcel Duchamp, To Be Looked a (from the Other Side of the Glass) with One Eye, Close to, for Almost an Hour, 1918 © 2000 Succession Marcel Duchamp, ARS, N.Y./ADAGP, Paris
6. http://www.toutfait.com/issues/issue_2/Notes/shambroom.html
7. Josephin Peladan, translator and editor, Leonard de Vinci, Traite de la Peinture (Paris: Librairie Delagrave, 1910), 113. English translations in A. Phillip McMahon, translator, Treatise on Painting by Leonardo da Vinci (Princeton: Princeton University Press, 1956), 177, and Edward MacCurdy, translator and editor, The Notebooks of Leonardo da Vinci (New York: George Braziller, 1954), 241.
8. http://en.wikipedia.org/wiki/Erik_Erikson
9. Jacques Villon and His Cubist Prints, I. H. Shoemaker, Philadelphia Museum of Art, 2001, ISBN: 0-87633-153-3
10. Transcription of a conversation between Michael Ayrton and Yehudi Menuhin, BBC, 1973
11. Art in America, Vol. 48, No. 3, 1960, page57
12. www. http://en.wikipedia.org/wiki/Louis_Vauxcelles
13. Poetry, Volume CC, No. 4, page 360

Jacques Villon's Cubist Work

But, is it Cubism?

I.
Non-imperative Categories

We encounter a problem when categorizing Villon's prints, drawings, and paintings as "Cubist." Humans like to categorize. It started with Aristotle and will not quit. We have a fondness for putting things neatly into boxes; but to do so runs the risk of mislabelling. For those in the psychology trades and the medical insurance trade, having a handy guide to what are blithely called mental disorders, is a real gift. The trades person need not spend too much time on considering her patient's chief "complaint" (as we used to call it in my medical days) but instead can readily bring to mind a box into which to place the unfortunate complainant, who, as likely as not, is reacting to the world's madness, which cannot be stopped, and who thereby needs our kindest response. Instead, the client, as s/he is now often labelled, enters another world, one of pharmacology, where, because one has been placed within a specific box, the pinball game of pill choosing begins. There are pills designed for each of the boxes; the next step is pretty easy. And the poor soul leaves with a prescription for pharmacologic side effects, which usually include significant weight gain. [By means of which sign, the poor soul knows the pill seems to be "working."]

I suppose when a label catches-on, one feels the urge to go with the flow. Thus even astute and innovative art critics use common terms as a shorthand for periods of art that are more or less understood. But, there is the rub, the 'more or less' part. There are assumptions made about the meaning of terms: fauvism, post-impressionism, impressionism, neo-impressionism, futurism, belle epoque, minimalism, primitivism, and finally, here for discussion, Cubism. Do we, do you, know exactly to what the term Cubism might apply? Do we apply the 'walks like a duck' test to a painting or drawing or are the criteria more precise? If the artist's work "looks" something like another artist's work, work which has already been so categorized, does that mean it should also be so called? This is a serious problem; a label carries a quality of worth. Men and women know this; some actually wear the label from an item of clothing so that it can readily be seen. Clothing manufacturers have carried this to ridiculous extremes, selling their clothing pre-marked, in very large letters, on the outside of the garment. In art, we have experienced this extreme: Warhol had a factory generate the "art" and it sold as long as it had his signature. In short, the signature became the value, not the work itself.

This diversion from the problems of art and art history into seemingly unrelated areas is meant quite seriously. I do not hold a PhD in art history, but I have advanced degrees in medicine and anatomy. And I have been an art collector for 65 years--I began with my first purchase at age 12. Furthermore, I have been "collecting" Villon for 42 years, during which time I have learned something, likely equal in breadth to a scholar's study of Villon's work. And, because I have limited my expertise to works on paper (not because I would not have wished to own several of his wonderful oil paintings) the limit forced me to stay focused upon the question at hand. One thing is quite clear to me: we should listen carefully, not to the critics and art historians, but rather to Villon himself, and, as well, to his younger brothers, Raymond Duchamp-Villon and Marcel Duchamp.

Both Duchamp and Villon denied they were doing "Cubist" work. The term Cubism started quite innocently: art critic Louis Vauxcelles described "bizarre cubiques" in a painting by Braque in 1908. Another critic, Louis Chassevent saw "cubes" in a painting by Metzinger. These referents are not, in fact, cubes but instead are flattened picture spaces influenced by the images of Cezanne. Once exploited, off-hand terms work their way into the parlance of the time. The coinages breed additional commentary, more categories and sub-categories as they grow in strength, to become food to nourish books, newspaper and magazine articles and, like the newly announced arrival of the "Higgs Boson (the "god" particle), they enter mainstream chatter. Denials are ignored.

2.
Villon and Villon

Gaston Duchamp, whom we know as Jacques Villon, fell under many social and intellectual influences. The choice of Villon for his surname, and "Jack," first, then later, Jacques, as his first, bear analysis. Francois Villon, the 15th century poet namesake chosen by Gaston, was a thief and vagabond. His "Grand Testament" is a poetic "will" in which he leaves to persons he has encountered in life a variety of good, and not so good, willings. Why would Gaston, who was quite shy, a somewhat reticent first child, one with a strong sense of responsibility, both to his parents and to his siblings, choose the name of a rather flamboyant bounder? Well, I do not know, but perhaps we can guess. We know that of the seven Duchamp children, only 6 made it to adulthood, the first Madeleine (a subsequent girl was also named Madeleine) died at age 3 when her mother, Lucie, was several months pregnant with Marcel, the fourth Duchamp child. Lucie Duchamp, the mother, was almost completely deaf by the time Marcel was born; the two older brothers, Gaston and Raymond were away at school. Marcel recalled that his mother was, at best, unusual, severely retiring; he feared her. What we know from psychological and sociological studies of birth order, "first" children, such as Gaston (Jacques Villon) tend to be reliable, conscientious, perfectionists who don't like surprises.

Guilliame Apollinaire, Villon, Gleizes, Duchamp, Duchamp-Villon, and a host of others gathered regularly at Puteaux,* which was Villon's life-long and final painting place, studio and home. And, they talked-- about painting, literature, poetry -- a real intellectual's delight.

Writing about Jacques Villon in 1964, Francis Steegmuller (1) reported "an undeniable spiritual kinship between himself and the poet Francois Villon. J. Villon is quoted: I felt that he and I had in common "l'amour pour une vie chaude, aimee pour elle meme," [love for a hot life, loved for itself] "evitant les conventions sociales, vie insouciante." [avoiding the social conventions, a carefree life] Out of delicacy, the artist always pronounced the name giving the two l's a pure "I" sound, and not the French "y" sound customarily used in pronouncing the name of the poet: "It seemed more respectful not to take over his name entirely." (2) (It might be noted here that Villon wasn't the poet's real name either: he was born Francois Corbeuil and took the name Villon from foster father, Guillaume de Villon, chaplain in the collegiate church of Saint-Benoît-le-Bestourne, and a professor of canon law, who took Villon into his house.) (3)

Raymond, who became a sculptor, was believed by Villon and by many others, to be the most talented of the four Duchamp artists (Gaston/Raymond/Marcel/Suzanne). His death in WWI, was unnecessary because he could have been exempted, for several reasons, from military service. Growing responsibilities fell to Gaston--Marcel left in 1915, avoiding the war's madness and the family's problems. There are, therefore, a number of competing and complementary reasons for life-long effects on the eldest son's personality. His successes in Paris as an illustrator, one with a wry sense of humor, eventuated not in his permanent displacement to the rich art influences of this city, but instead, found him returning to Puteaux, to an isolated studio, where he remained for his life.**

*When I first heard of Puteaux in relation to Villon, I imagined it a countryside harbor, well away from the bustle of Paris and all it meant to the artists of Montparnasse of Bateau-Lavoir and elsewhere. It is in fact only about 5 miles from the center of Paris. So much for wool gathering!

**Art historians commonly assert this: that Villon moved to his 'isolated' studio, an image that suggests distance and solitude. In fact, as above, Puteaux was as easy to visit from Paris as Harlem or Brooklyn might be from downtown Manhattan.

3.
The Duchamps Speak

Villon compared Marcel to himself as 'porcelain to my stoneware.' Marcel's intellect and innate tendency to doubt the prevailing views of most everything shaped Villon. To Villon's preference for da Vinci's ideas of pyramids as basic elements in composition, Marcel countered, provoking, with this sneering image: see page 4. Duchamp was resentful of the "art world." Most of his famous gestures derided the prevailing art culture. His passion was for the game of chess, which he played at expert level. His game with life was similarly played. Duchamp had a life-long influence upon Villon; Villon must have considered him in almost every stroke of his brush?

Villon's "Cubist" forays embrace several theories which he formulated under the influence of his education, his family, his deep interest in poetry, especially the poetry of the symbolists, the intellectual intercourse that took place at Puteaux, his early experiences as a draftsman and illustrator, and finally, the landscape of the French countryside where his life took him.

Taking these, more or less in order, the intellectual demands of his schooling are well known. His early studies at the Lycee Corneille (In Rouen) were exceedingly rigorous, consisting of Latin, Greek, English or German, philosophy, history, rhetoric, science, mathematics, and drawing lessons from Philippe Zacharie (who also taught at Rouen's Ecole des Beaux-Arts, where Villon (and Raymond) also studied. Villon developed a "fluid and incisive" drawing style, much admired by Marcel. After a year in the Army, where he received training in the art of camouflage, which included a close study of theories of color, he moved to Paris and Montmartre where he lived the artist's life and made a living doing commercial work shown throughout Paris on billboards and in newspapers alongside of those of Cheret, Mucha and Toulouse-Lautrec. (4)

Villon's father was a notary, one of the most influential and important positions in Blainville's daily life in those days. He acted as a community advice giver, collector of debts, drawer of wills and contracts, collector of taxes and arbitrator of disputes. He was a small and energetic man whom Tomkins (4) describes as a good listener, possessing a cheerful, alert, nimble mind. He wished for Gaston to follow him in the study of the Law, and although the boy agreed to study as his father wished, he bargained for joint study of art, which eventually won out. As a foil to his dour and withdrawn mother, his father Eugene Duchamp must have stood-out as a strong and demanding influence. It is thought that Gaston chose a pseudonym so as not to embarrass his father by his humorous illustrations which appeared not only on billboards (signed) but also in publications such as Le Rire (Laughter-a humor magazine), Le Courrier Francais (a light and satirical newspaper).

The influences of Raymond and Marcel were very important. In 1906, Villon moved permanently to Puteaux. He described his reasons to do so to Dora Vallier: "If I hadn't left Montmartre then I wouldn't have done a thing in the whole of my life — which means I would have kept turning out cartoons and engravings. Up in Montmartre, someone would always pop in just to smoke a pipe and I was surrounded by too many boys who had already given up the hope of making something out of their lives. I was feeling the need of leaving the newspapers and giving the whole of my time to painting. Eventually I did that but it was four years later, in 1910."(5)

After moving to Puteaux, he became much closer to his brother, Raymond, who had given-up his study of medicine and was living close-by in Neuilly. They began to frequently see each other. Raymond's temperament, which was dynamic and emotional, seemed to influence Villon's resolve to paint. Weekly, a group of artists and poets met at Gleizes' studio (in nearby Courbevoie) on Mondays at and on Sundays at Puteaux. The group included Villon, Duchamp, Raymond, Suzanne, Metzinger, Picabia, Leger, Appolinaire, and others. It was a highly intellectual, technically skilled group which shared and discussed ideas about sculpture, painting, and social movements. Raymond became increasingly influential. He was in charge of hanging at the 1911 Salon D'Automne where the group's paintings were displayed. Villon was influenced not by Raymond's art, so much as by his brother's enthusiasm. (5)

Villon (JV) speaks about Marcel--from his 1957 interview with Dora Vallier(DV):

> JV: "Very often I feel in Marcel... how should I put it?--family gestures and attitudes. I was twelve years old when he was born; he has grown up under my eyes."

> DV: "Marcel, who "does everything as if all that matters is to make some use of time that goes by", Marcel who "when one of his 'Formes Maliques', done in glass before 1914, breaks to pieces exclaims: "At last!" as if all this time he had been waiting only for the day when the whole of his work were to disappear", Marcel, who "plays chess with relentless eagerness" hoping that the day will come when he will be able to guess from the first movement the entire development of the game, Marcel Duchamp, Dada in the marrow of his bones, is he not a part of Jacques Villon?"

> JV: "I know only too well that art is a game and that it is bound to perish but all the same I love reaching for the further end of creation."

Villon's education at the Lycee Corneille had a notable influence upon him. As a young man, he was already acquainted with Francois Villon's 15th century poetry and its special meaning for him. The larger than life presence of Guilliame Appolinaire (born Wilhelm Albert Włodzimierz Apolinary Kostrowicki), a man with far reaching influences upon a host of artistic and literary movements, including "Futurism," "Cubism," "Dada," and "Surrealism," must have been exciting, stimulating and personally influential to Villon. Villon's close artistic connections to symbolist poets and their philosophies also relate to the meetings in Puteaux and Courbevoie.*** Indeed, the intellectual aspect of art, above and beyond the "retinal," became of major importance to Villon. One can see it, even in his earliest work. Some might dismiss his illustrations as cartoons; but, cartoons are the essence of much significant art, surely Goya's and Picasso's. One of Villon's cherished hopes was to induce, through his paintings, an intellectual journey to be taken by the viewer. Like the symbolist poet, the idea is not to reveal everything with obvious clarity, but rather to make the viewer, the reader, work for the solution.

Villon's interest in poetry and poets was not limited to his adopted namesake. The poetry of Stephane Malarmé and Paul Valéry--the philosophical substance which drove it--impacted the art of Villon and his brothers.

Paul Valéry, who "has been called the greatest poet [of the first half of the 20th Century]. . . was almost completely the intellectual, mistrusting anything but conscious and deliberate effort and denying that the spontaneous was truly creative." Valéry had published, in 1895, his "Introduction to the Method of Leonardo da Vinci." All concepts of Cubism and geometric abstract art are found there. In an essay about Malarmé, Valéry described the seminal influence Stephane Malarmé's writing had upon him: "I came to the conclusion that there was an inner system in Mallarmé, a system which could be distinguished from philosophy, and moreover from mysticism; but not unanalogous to it. I believed, rather more accurately, that a work resolutely thought out and sought for in the hazards of the mind, systematically, and through a determined analysis of definite and previously prescribed conditions, whatever its value might be once it had been produced, did not leave the mind of its creator without having modified him, and forced him to recognize and in some way to reorganize himself. I said to myself that it was not the accomplished work, and its appearance and effect in the world, that can fulfil and edify us; but only the way in which we have done it. Art and its difficulties increase our stature; but the Muses and good fortune only visit us to leave us again." (6)

Malarmé wrote a statement about the new poetry of "the school of 1885," that included Verlaine and Rimbaud: "The contemplation of objects, the image that rises out of the reverie the objects provoke—those are the song. But the Parnassians take the thing in its entirety and point at it: thereby they lack mystery. They deprive the reader of the delightful illusion that he is a creator. To name an object is to destroy three-quarters of our pleasure in a poem—the joy of guessing, step by step. The ideal is to suggest the object. We derive the most from the mystery that constitutes the symbol when we evoke the object step by step in order to portray a state of mind. Or, the other way round, when we choose an object and derive a state of mind from it by a sequence of decipherings."

This statement bears a remarkable resemblance to Villon's own description of his method of work: "In composing a painting I always begin with a proportion which I then plot. My starting point is in nature, but I don't feel the need of sticking to nature. My painting's got to be my creation. But instead of relying on chances, I make sure that I have something certain, a proportion on which I can base myself. Then I move a step further. I divide the canvas and once this is done, the canvas begins to take shape. Sometimes I leave till the very end, quite visible, all these lines of subdivision which may be called the regulating plot. In this way I can rely on their lead as I move along". Villon confesses: "Chance frightens me."

Throughout his long painting and drafting career, Villon stuck to a group of influences that included theoretical ideas about representation of the world in a painting, etching or drawing. High among these was the influence of Leonard da Vinci's book: Treatise on Painting.

> JV: "This art consists in painting through pyramids all forms and colours of the contemplated objects. I say through pyramids because however small an object might be, it will be still greater than the summit point of this pyramid. Therefore, if you take the lines on the edges of each body and you continue them to an unique point, they will go in a pyramidal direction" (7)

> JV: "In 1908 I was relying greatly on quick sketches for my paintings. What was then capturing my attention was the line of intention, the inner line of a movement — and that enabled me to find, as for instance in "Les Haleurs" [The Barge Haulers] a synthesis of movement."

> "People are wrong in comparing me to the Futurists. To begin with, I didn't know them and then — and this is what really matters — they conceive movement as being decomposed in successive jumps, which is a downright cinematographic device, while I aim to convey the synthesis of movement through an uninterrupted continuity."

Note that both the "Futurist" conception (above) and also the common understanding of the "Cubist" conception (seeing a thing from all sides at once) differ in a significant way from the goals of both Villon and his brother, Marcel--for example: Nude Descending the Staircase. This painting in the view of the two Duchamps presents continuous, all at once, movement; it is neither the Cubist (all sides at once) nor the separate jumps of futurism. The precepts of the Technical Manifesto of Futurist Painting explain that, "On account of the persistency of an image upon the retina, moving objects constantly multiply themselves; their form changes like rapid vibrations, in their mad career. Thus a running horse has not four legs, but twenty, and their movements are triangular."(8) This was not the intention of Villon and Marcel.

> "Till about 1910, I painted as the birds sing, following my instinct, without thinking too much."

> "I remember that about 1911, we used sometimes to say, for instance, that if the Baudelaire's bust [by Raymond] were to explode, it would do so along certain lines of force. Therefore, the lines of force represent the object grasped in its middle, thus defining its form. They could be either merely traced or stressed through coloured ground-lights."

> JV: "After 1914 I began to treat objects through their different planes. Like a good boy at school I drew the same object full face, profile and three quarters. In other words I couldn't begin a painting unless I had made the complete circle around the object — and it was all too long."

If drawing comes much more freely into Villon's painting, it has still to fulfil a curious mission: instead of being an introduction to the picture, it becomes the picture's conclusion:

"Sometimes, over the colours, I redo my picture in ink. It is an accompaniment. The work is already composed and the accompaniment can be quite free without doing much harm.   And a bit of my heart can then go into it."

DV: ""Painting is a matter of thought" admonished Leonardo, but we have forgotten it long ago. The whole of modern art — and for perfectly plausible reasons at that — addresses our senses as if its only intention were to shatter the categories of the mind. But Villon's art does not yield to the eyes unless it is first approached by the mind — and this may well explain why our time has been so slow in recognising Villon. Left on its own in front of this art, without the support of the mind, the sight cannot embrace its exceptional amplitude. Unable to perceive what has provoked the forms, the eyes are easily dazzled by the shimmer of the colours, thus misguiding our appreciation and forcing us quite often to ask: "Why this evanescent halo, why this refusal to form?" This, however, would be a false conclusion born out of a partial use of our faculties. Villon's art may well offer itself to our eyes and our affection, as does modern painting on the whole. Yet we have to discover it in its particular order, if we want it to unfold and open without reservations."

JV: "I avoid good taste. I do my very best to avoid it. I never put a line or a colour without a reason, an interior reason linking with that other reason which is inside myself. If good taste were to come into it, all one could do would be to add up other elements while — and it's taken me quite a while to see it — it is the foresight that brings the picture to an end".

JV: "I want to reduce everything to the absolute."

Villon's art is unique because of the theoretical foundation which bases it. His methods flow from a deep knowledge of the technology and physics of his materials. Here is how he says it:

JV: "Not only are the colours from the tubes different from the colours-light (colours of light), but there is also a world of difference in the way colours from the tube and those of light link among themselves. For instance, once I have laid the very first tone, which is taken from the local one [his palette], I have no idea which colours are going to follow. It's not up to me to choose. The chromatic circle is going to show them to me, because the chromatic circle on which hues of light and their nuances are set in perfect order, has been so calculated that one can tell how these hues link together. In this way, when I have found on the chromatic circle the two colours that go on both sides of my first tone, all I have to do is to go all over again through the same operation. First I take one of these two colours, then the other and each one, according to its position in the chromatic circle, brings two new colours on to the canvas. In this way, all colours come to be located in the picture according to their interferences in the light and the surface covered by each one of them depends on the positioning of the planes in relation to the source of light. There are always different planes — don't you think so? There is one that comes forward followed by another one while a third remains further back... On the canvas they overlap, but their intersections are always there and they reveal the planes and assign to each colour its precise place."

*** Courbevoie is also about 5 miles from center Paris and is about 1.6 miles from Puteaux. The two locations were the meeting place for the artists and poets known to Villon.

4.
Dada and Beyond

Richard Heulsenbeck, co-founder of Dada, a gifted psychoanalyst and art historian, describes the position of modern art at the time of Villon as a psychic state of:

"special awareness of man's situation as a human being. (9) Though it is, of course, not a new situation, there is a higher awareness of the play between the creative and the destructive forces at this moment in history. This awareness expresses itself in radically new modes. Of these, abstraction is not the most characteristic mode, but it is a particularly interesting one. Its fractionalization, elimination of the object, its abolishment of perspective, and its denial of beauty all express this higher awareness. Much of abstract art, like other modes of modern art, cannot be judged by the old standards of beauty. The concept of beauty seems to have suffered particularly from man's new awareness of la condition humaine."

"...When, in the isolation of country life in southern France, Cezanne suddenly became dissatisfied with conventional aesthetic expression, he had reached this breaking point. He said he felt rationality and irrationality, being and nonbeing, the creative and the destructive forces, the subjective and the objective, colliding within him. He wanted badly to find the "objective" in art. What he found by giving in to this fractionalizing, destructive, creative trend was a new reality, *la realite nouvelle*. Aesthetically and psychologically, he found a new world where the forces within him could achieve a new balance. [Cezanne's search for the "objective" seems akin to Villon's search for the "absolute."]

"...When Cezanne decided that life and the world of ordinary reality should not be copied, but should instead be structuralized, he started a trend that has not yet come to an end. This structuralizing is partly an expression of man's new fractionalizing attitude toward the world; therefore it is negative and a part of nonbeing. But structure is also construction; therefore it is a part of the positive and the creative that leads to the experience of transcendence that we have been discussing.

...Though the impressionists had said they were interested in the way things change under the changing light, it was not really a question of optics that drove them on; it was the urge to find the thing behind the thing. In this sense, their work was not unlike Cezanne's. Though Cezanne denounced impressionism, he also wanted to see behind the thing. He was concerned with the "essence" of things, and light with its various shades was, he felt, an outside phenomenon. The structural secret became the secret of creation because it seems to answer the question: How is the thing made?

Heulsenbeck reaffirms that Cezanne is the real father of modern painting. Villon obtained much of his theoretical ideas from Cezanne, either directly or through the discussions that took place in Puteaux and environs. Villon continues to describe his painting experiences:

JV: "Now, as far as colours are concerned, to obtain the hues of light, I break down each colour with some white, still keeping an eye on the chromatic circle. To obtain their untarnished purity, I use a palette of oil-impregnated paper which I throw away once I have finished. Before putting any colour on the canvas, I make a separate mixture for each colour. In a way, I am preparing a brand new palette. Once the mixture is ready, once I have obtained the tone-value I need, I compare it once again with the chromatic circle before transferring it on to the canvas."

"In the Middle Ages they used to recite a prayer before starting work on a painting. Much in the same way, I lean on the golden section to get my initial assurance."

"When I make direct studies, my drawings follow the inner movement, the inner line of the object which, like a tight rope, determines its unity. In other words, I make an analysis straight from nature, so that I may have the time to think it over."

"When I engrave, I can't very well put-in a regulating plot. But it doesn't mean that I dive into the unknown. I make a lot of drawings before getting hold of the copper plate in order to avoid any unpleasant surprise at the last moment."

"Sketches always give me something, an impulse towards something. Very often I get the general movement of a picture from a mere note in the sketchbook. Many times, taking another look at drawings which I had thought pretty useless while doing them, I discover in them another meaning, as if they were a kind of creation. So I force myself to keep on drawing even when I don't feel the slightest desire to do so."

"I was interested in Toulouse-Lautrec's way of painting. I remember also seeing about the same time some drawings of his. A journalist from Rouen had arranged a little show in a colour man's shop — a real colour man, I mean — hoping to sell a few of them." [Colour man = dealer in colors and paints]

"At that time, I was already quite struck by Impressionism. A few painters in Rouen even were influenced by it. I liked their work because I felt that it was a break from official painting. What I liked in the Impressionist pictures was the minute touch which isn't aggressive at all and I have used it in some of my early works. But I must say that it was Neo-Impressionism that got under my skin. It was still in Rouen that I saw for the first time an exhibition of Neo-Impressionist paintings. At that time, I hadn't a clue of the scientific side, but I was deeply impressed by the atmosphere of these paintings. I didn't suspect in the least that there could be a science of painting, a science of colour. I can kick myself for having been so careless at that time."

5.
Ratiocination

Questions have arisen regarding the influence of the Golden Ratio or Section d'Or upon Villon. I suspect there was less of a wholesale adoption of the numerical equivalence of this geometric relationship than there was an acceptance of the theoretical possibilities inherent in, for example, da Vinci's reference to this entity in his "Treatise on Painting," (7) After all, the kettle of knowledge of modern science, of modern painting was at the boil; these painters, who grouped together at regular intervals in Puteaux, and up the road a way at Gleize's studio in Courbevoie, were highly intelligent, intellectually capable men who cared deeply for their work and for its meaning within the context of the history that impinged upon and instructed them.

Is it possible to find credence for the 'golden section,' the golden ratio, Phi, in any of Villon's work? I mean evidence that would stand the test of empiricism, of mathematical analysis. Can we find any measurements which might suggest that he was relying upon the fact that, in a triangular form, the ratio of the altitude to the base was 1.618? Or, in a rectangle, the ratio of the short side to the long side was equal to 1.618, this number being the Golden Ratio or Phi or the "Section d'Or." I think not. I believe it a mistake to reduce Villon and his fellow painters in the group to this title, to mere geometers. Furthermore, even the second of his first two etchings, made when he was 16, shows triangular forms which, by a stretch, might be understood (or interpreted, perhaps, in a Procrustean sense) as evidence for this theoretical bent. But the work preceded any association with the name: Section d'Or by many (16) years. Villon describes his own recollections of Section d'Or:

> JV: "To begin with, I claim the paternity of this title (Section d'Or). In 1912 our works were again shown together in a Gallery in rue La Boetie: this was the first exhibition of the Section d'Or. In our talks, we came to discuss more and more frequently the organisation of a picture. So the idea that a picture has to be reasoned before being actually painted got anchored in our minds. We knew nothing of the problem of the golden section in the philosophy of the Ancient Greeks. I read the "Treatise on Painting" by Leonardo and I realised the importance he was attributing to the golden section. But it was mainly in discussing that we clarified our ideas, without over-burdening ourselves with science".

I emphasize the importance of Villon's confession. The meaning of the golden ratio to Greek mathematicians differs from that of the painter. He confesses his own (and fellow painter's) lack of application of the necessary scientific (or mathematical) details to works of art—to paintings and etchings; to them the phrase became a kind of word dalliance.

I have considered in detail the Section d'Or or golden ratio title, to which Villon claims paternity. Along with Leonardo's ideas about pyramidal shapes, the search for mathematical 'absolutes,' and extensive preparatory planning, the ideal, Section d'Or, is simply another element of the method Villon uses to portray his object. Its usage is not mathematical, rather it is metaphorical. Furthermore, as we are reminded by D'Arsay Thompson (10), there are many "examples of bad reasoning as are often to be met within writings relating to mathematical subjects." Mario Livio, in his book, The Golden Ratio, and others who have questioned finding this ratio in Greek architecture and Egyptian pyramids, point to the imprecise applications of post-hoc measurements. (11) I know from my experience in drawing over the past ten years that I often find myself making triangular shapes, of which some approach "gold."

> JV "If I have painted or I paint abstract pictures, it is because my painting has seemed or seems to me almost photographic. Only I find that abstract art does not offer enough difficulties to overcome and enough depth to re-discover. I would like to reach abstract art but with clear cut reasons. I would like to reach such a consistent simplification that it could receive any punch from the outside without losing its supreme balance."

Villon is opposed to automaticity. In this way he is anti-Stein (Gertrude) and pro-Mallarmé or pro-Valéry. By succumbing to intuition or automatic painting, he feels there is a loss of the influence of the human intellect. As stated by Valéry in his essay on Mallarmé, the search for the hidden in a work demands such intense intellectual effort that the outcome of such effort is improvement in the seeker.

What we have in Villon is an engraver, draughtsman and painter whose work was concerned with a poetic theory of the movements of the object conceived, not in a cinematic frame-by-frame sense, but rather in Villon's idea of the absolute. To Villon, the absolute is the all-at-once three dimensional object, deconstructed and abstracted to show only the essential portions. Those parts and abstractions are painted, drawn or engraved as color, form, and line. The final work allows an observer with sufficient intellectual capacity, one willing to leave visual prejudices behind, an opportunity to see what is really there. With combined efforts -- the mind of the artist who is armed with a plan, and the efforts of the witness -- the hidden (but not really hidden) object becomes revealed. It is like a poem, "Vae Soli," by Guillaume Apollinaire, that Steegmuller (1) comments upon: "It would be difficult to find a poem that fits more exactly than Vae Soli, the requirements of Symbolism as stated by Mallarmé, "to name an object is to destroy three-quarters of our pleasure in a poem—the joy of guessing, step-by-step. The ideal is to suggest the object. . ." It is this symbolism that exists in the whole of Villon's work. And, in the Cubism of early Picasso and Braque it is certainly there. Of all the so-called Cubists, only Villon and Mondrian, especially Mondrian, carried the theory to its own logical place.

Mondrian felt that the Cubists were unwilling to "pursue the logical consequences of their own visual audacity." Cubist theory was essentially abandoned by Picasso and Braque who followed a more graspable image path, a safer one, which, although not purely representational, usually left enough of an object in the work to allow ready recognition. Mondrian, however, abandoned completely any reference to subject, to reality based subject, using instead, metaphorical weighting of primary colors and linear formality to allow the mind to suggest the meaning, if any.

Marcel Duchamp adopts an even more rigorous aversion to "art" as a reflection of the times. The technological changes brought to industry create mass produced items that have all of the characteristics of fine, indeed, wondrous works of art. So Marcel Duchamp simply chooses an object from the products and presents it as a work of art--thereby defying expectation and reifying his belief that the world is manifesting entropy--it is descending into a chaos from which a search for the "absolute" underlying an artistic subject no longer satisfies his sensitive mind. He retreats into a world of tautological absurdity--he tries to find in chess a foil for the madness of the world, a game he can control versus a world he cannot. His life, then, becomes a work of art. Marcel, who once shared the urge to theorize and to let theories become manifest in painting, breaks, artistically, from his brother--amicably, of course, but indeed, it is a real break.

To more conclusively demonstrate that Villon did not use the golden ratio, Phi, as his layout guide, refer to page 21.

6.
A Cube by Another Name

So, Cubism? Is there really such a thing? I am not convinced of Villon's intention to join the movement that is called Cubism by . . .

By whom?

Is that not really the question we should be asking? Into what formula or group of conditions is it possible for an art historian or critic to insert Villon and thereby to call a period of his work Cubist? There are no cubes in his work, just as there were none in Braque's nor Picasso's. The triangular and pyramidal structures Villon makes a part of his images originate either de novo (see his work at age 16) or through influences from Leonardo. Villon claims to be the father of the term "Section D'or" nonetheless, he denies attributing to this mathematical (or scientific) ratio a theoretical foundation for his work.

Finally, Cubism has come to be associated with a specific period of time, the 1910's and 1920's. Probably originating as a critic's remark in 1908, image shapes characterizing this brief episode are generally understood as terminating around 1915. Some claim it was never terminated completely. But claims of this kind are outliers. Whether or not one chooses to place Villon in the bin of Cubism, it is clear from a study of his work that whatever his images be called, he continued to do similar ones and variations through-out his lifetime. His preferred shapes presaged for him that he might be so categorized, for they began with his earliest work. Thus, should we label Villon a ProtoCubist, a Cubist, or, finally, a Post-modern Cubist?

> What's in a name? that which we call a rose
> By any other name would smell as sweet;

(1) Jacques Villon, Master Printmaker. An exhibition at R.M. Light & Co., Helene C. Seiferheld Gallery inc., New York, February, 1964. (New York: High Grade Press, 1964)

(2) Jacques Villon and His Cubist Prints, Innis Howe Shoemaker, Philadelphia Museum of Art, 2001, ISBN: 0-87633-153-3

(3) http://en.wikipedia.org/wiki/Fran%C3%A7ois_Villon

(4) Calvin Tomkins, Duchamp: A Biography, Henry Holt, Nov. 1996, ISBN: 978-0805057898 (paperback

edition, 2008)

(5) Jacques Villon: Oeuvres De 1897 a 1956, Dora Vallier, Editions Cahiers D'art (1957)

(6) Paul Valéry, Selected Writings, New Directions Publishing corp., New York, 1964,
ISBN: 978- 0-8112-0213-8

(7) Treatise on Painting, by Leonardo da Vinci, par. 201

(8) http://www.unknown.nu/futurism/techpaint.html

(9) Memoirs of a Dada Drummer, Richard Heulsenbeck, New York, Viking Press, 1974
ISBN: 0-520-07370-3

(10) On Growth and Form, D'Arcy Thompson, Dover Publications, Mineola, NY, 1992
ISBN: 0-486-67135-6 p. 112

(11) The Golden Ratio: The Story of Phi, the World's Most Astonishing Number, Mario Livio, Broadway Publications, 2002,
ISBN: 0-767-90815-5

Note: Villon shows us his working method in the following print. The "layout" is designed using rectangles. Further, the rectangles are grouped into a larger rectangular formation. Each of the smaller rectangles is divided on the diagonal into triangles which resemble, superficially, the triangle which is the manifestation of the Phi ratio, the "golden" ratio. If we measure the base and the altitude of the rectangles we should be able to approach 1.618 if Villon is using the "golden" ratio as his guide. We can do the same calculation with the larger rectangle. For the triangles, we obtain 1.37 and for the large rectangle, 1.22. Even by a Procrustean stretch, these figures do not support Phi as a guiding ratio.

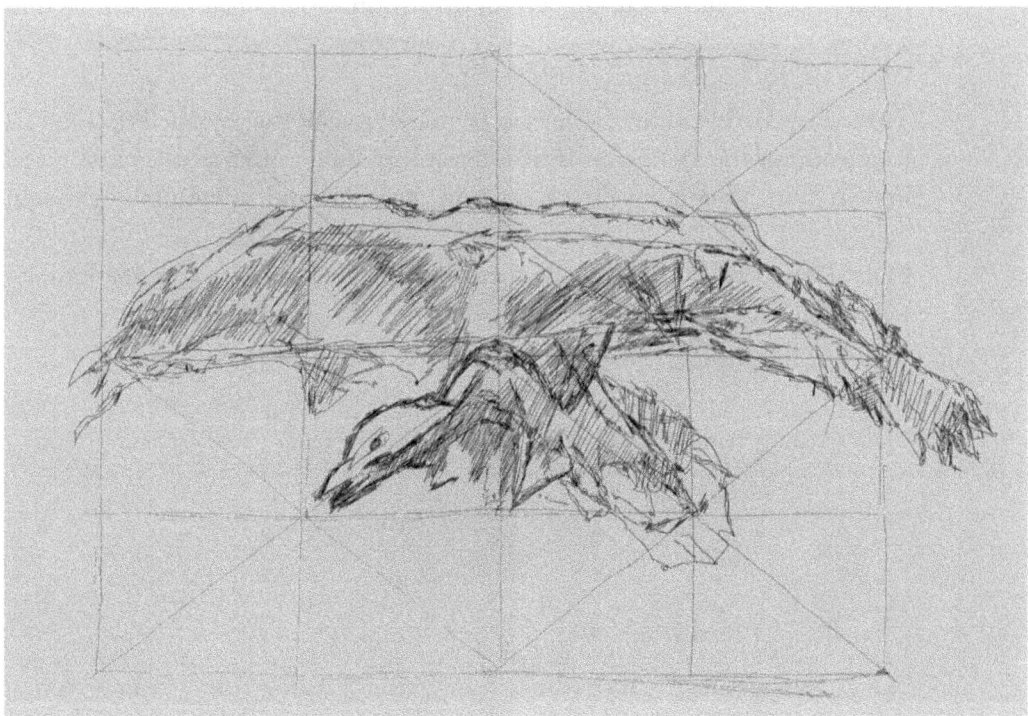

1962 "L'Epervier" Etching, hard ground, to illustrate Hesiod, "Work and Days," No. 92 of an edition of 180, 10-1/2 x 16 inches.

The Women From Thrace

G&P, 1979: Etching, signed on the plate.
First state, a few experimental proofs; final state, thirty proofs. The proof we can find at the B. N. is annotated as: second and last state, rolled up.

Exhibitions: Galerie L. Goldschmidt, New York 1955, No. 16; Rath Museum, Geneva 1955, No. 110; B.N. , Paris 1959, No. 48; Stockholm 1960s, No. 102; M.D.C. , Le Havre 1962, No. 8; Museum of Fine Arts, Boston 1964, No. 35; Gallery Light, New York 1966, No. 22; Lisbon 1966, No. 3; Chicago 1967, No. 26. ; Gallery L. Goldschmidt, New York 1970, No. 75.

Bibliography: A&P, 1950 No. 119; cat. Hotel Drouot, Paris 1958, No. 64, 1962, No. 18.
1. MFAB, No.35.
2. AIC, No. 19.
3. LGI, 1970, No. 75.
4. RSJ 1967, No. 26 (Artist's Proof).
5. RSJ 1975, No. 49.
6. MMS, 1960, No. 102.
7. RMA, 1984, No. 46, pict. p 53.
8. RSJ, 1989B, No. 44.
9. RSJ, 1991, No. 47.

Technique: This is pure "hard ground" etching. A material resistant to acid, is spread on the metal plate and allowed to dry. When dry, the material is hard and can be sharply incised with a point.

Time: The Art Institute of Chicago owns a watercolor with pencil drawing that is a preparatory work for this etching. It is of interest that Villon often worked first in painting or drawing, often with a definitive work resulting, before he did any prints of the subject.

Note: I have two of this series in the collection. See page 66, The Work of Jacques Villon, Leissring, 2011

1907 Les Femmes de Thrace

Type:	Etching, Hard Ground
Reference:	G&P: E 205 ii/ii
Edition/Number:	30/22
Size--H, W:	8.5 x 6 inches
Framed:	Yes
Inventory Number:	JCL0657-JCL0131
Provenance:	Annex Gallery--11/15/1988

Three Women On The Grass or Resting On The Grass

G&P, 1979: Etching, signed on the plate.
Some proofs justified on thirty, others on fifty; On one proof there is writing: Proof done with a wet cloth.

Exhibitions: Galerie Louis Square, Paris 1954, No. 18; Antwerp 1955, No. 170; Rath Museum, Geneva 1955, No. 109; Oslo 1958, No. 12; French Institute, Athens 1958; B.N., Paris 1959, No. 47; Gallery Light, New York 1966, No. 21; Chicago 1967, No. 114 ; Gallery L. Goldschmidt, New York 1970 No. 74.

Bibliography: A&P No. 118

1. L&S, 1964, No. 21.
2. LGI 1970, No. 74. (annotated by Villon: "éprouve retrouvée")
3. RSJ, 1967, No. 25. (Marked "Proof done with wet cloth")
4. RSJ, 1975, No. 48.
5. AIC, 1976, No. 19.

Technique: This is a hard ground etching; this print is annotated by Villon: "éprouve retrouvée," suggesting that it is the image referred to in the Goldschmidt catalogue. Both G&P and Goldschmidt state that there may be differing justifications, some based on 50 and others on 30.

Time: This is again Puteaux and his new studio. It is not known who the models are.

Note: Goldschmidt quotes the catalogue from Louis Carré, Paris, 1954:
  "...this is one of the first plates of Villon "where he recreates rather than describes the distribution of light and shadow.""

1907 Tres Femmes sur l'Herbe

Type:	Etching
Reference:	G&P: E203
Edition/Number:	30 or 50--artist's proof
Size--H, W:	6 -5/8 x 9 inches
Framed:	Yes
Inventory Number:	JCL 0658
Provenance:	Annex Gallery (11/15/1988)

The Dairy Maid

G&P, 1979: signed on the plate. First state, contours evoked in dry point, a proof resumed in lead pencil (B.N.); 2nd state, new work to the Etching, few proofs; final state, a few proofs in 1907; X No. (?) proofs signed, printed in 1960 and 60 proofs unsigned done in 1966 for the Guild of Engraving, Lausanne. Copper has been scratched.

Exhibition: Gallery G. Cramer, Geneva 1967, II, No. 3.

Bibliography: Non-described in A&P; cat. of the Gallery La Gravure, Lausanne, No. 9.

Technique: Hard ground etching.

Time: Villon favors the illustrative mode. This work is probably from the 1966 printing of the guild in Lausanne. Pencil annotated LL "15/60"

1907 "La Laitiere"

Type:	Etching
Reference:	G&P: E207
Edition/Number:	60 / 15
Size--H, W:	6-1/2 x 8 inches
Framed:	Matted
Inventory Number:	JCL0731
Provenance:	W. F. Maibaum Fine Art (6/11/1991)

Three Women On The Grass
or Resting On The Grass

G&P, 1979: Etching, signed on the plate.
Some proofs justified on thirty, others on fifty; On one proof there is writing: Proof done with a wet cloth.

Exhibitions: Galerie Louis Square, Paris 1954, No. 18; Antwerp 1955, No. 170; Rath Museum, Geneva 1955, No. 109; Oslo 1958, No. 12; French Institute, Athens 1958; B.N., Paris 1959, No. 47; Gallery Light, New York 1966, No. 21; Chicago 1967, No. 114 ; Gallery L. Goldschmidt, New York 1970 No. 74.

Bibliography: A&P. No. 118.

1. Light and Seiferheld, 1964, No. 21.
2. Goldschmidt, 1970, No. 74. (annotated by Villon: "éprouve retrouvée")
3. R. S. Johnson, 1967, No. 25. (Marked "Proof done with wet cloth")
4. R. S. Johnson, 1975, No. 48.
5. Art Institute of Chicago, 1976, No. 19.
6. RMA, 1984, No. 45.

Technique: This is a hard ground etching; this print is annotated by Villon: "ép d. artiste." Both G&P and Goldschmidt state that there may be differing justifications, some based on 50 and others on 30. Annotated LL, signed LR.

Time: This is again Puteaux and his new studio. It is not known who the models are.

Note: Goldschmidt quotes the catalogue from Louis Carré, Paris, 1954:
 "...this is one of the first plates of Villon "where he recreates rather than describes the distribution of light and shadow."" The long hatching lines and the absence of background distractions intensity the image.

1907 "Trois Femmes sur l'Herbe"

Type: Etching
Reference: G&P: E203
Edition/Number: 30 or 50 / proof
Size--H, W: 6-5/8 x 9 inches
Framed: Matted
Inventory Number: JCL2164
Provenance: Annex Gallery # MA 102 (4/7/1994)

Madeleine in the chair or Little Mutine

G&P, 1979: Drypoint. First state, before drypoint, a few proofs; 2nd state trimmed and suppression of a lot of work in between the girl's legs, before signature, a few proofs; Final state signature and date engraved. Edition of 25.

Exhibition: Chicago 1967, No. 37.

Bibliography: A&P. No. 146 ; cat. Hotel Drouot, Paris, February 1972, No. 182.

Technique: drypoint.

Time: The model is his sister, Madeleine (also known as Magdeleine) who was born in 1898 and who would be about 10 years old in this print. Mutine must have been his nickname for the girl. The family had many terms they shared, often as a secret language.

Note: There was a sister, Madeleine, who died at age three of a respiratory disease. She just preceded Marcel. The mother's grief was very significant. She dressed the young Marcel in very girlish clothing when he was young.

This engraving was based upon an illustration in Courier Francais, No. 8, February 18, 1909 "Oh! My vehicle, I am lost because it prevented me going in an omnibus."

I 296.

1908 "Madeleine au Fauteuil"

Type:	Drypoint
Reference:	G&P: E226 iii/iii
Edition/Number:	25 / 2
Size--H, W:	15-1/2 x 12 inches
Framed:	Matted
Inventory Number:	JCL2092
Provenance:	Lucien Goldschmidt/W. F. Maibaum (7/27/89)

The Hat Pin or Pinning the Hat

G&P, 1979: Dry Point; Twenty proofs.

Bibliography: A&P, 1950 No. 160.

1. RSJ, 1978, No. 31.
2. RMA, 1984, No. 50, pict. p. 56.

Technique: drypoint; again this amounts to drawing directly upon the copper plate with a sharp tool or diamond point. The ink is wiped into the grooves and the plate then wiped free of the ink to the extent that the artist chooses. Classical techniques employed the hand as the wiper.

Time: there is a noticeable change in the structure of Villon's images, perhaps beginning as early as this print. A certain angularity is beginning, almost an antecedent to his interest in Cubism. The absence of background detail is also apparent.

1909 "L'Epingle a Chapeau"

Type:	Drypoint
Reference:	G&P: E242
Edition/Number:	20 / 13
Size--H, W:	15-1/2 x 12 inches
Framed:	Yes
Inventory Number:	JCL0119
Provenance:	R. S. Johnson International, Chicago, Il

Nude standing with arms in the air.

G&P, 1979: Etching and Drypoint, signed on the plate.
Edition of 23; plate destroyed. Renée is the model. Villon and Duchamp must have used the same model. You can find her in the same pose in Marcel Duchamp's 1911 painting:"Jeune Homme et Jeune Fille dans le Printemps" and in a sketch of the same year.

Exhibitions: Museum of Modem Art, New York 1953, No. 35; Gallery Louis Square, Paris 1954, No. 21; Antwerp 1955, No. 172; Rath Museum, Geneva 1955, No. 136; B.N. , Paris 1959, No. 49; M. D. C. The Havre 1962, No. 9; Gallery Louis Square, Paris 1963, No. 3; Museum of Fine Arts, Boston 1964, No. 41 ; Gallery Light, New York 1964, No. 25; Chicago 1967, No. 43; Gallery L. Goldschmidt, New York 1970, No. 43; Museum of Fine Arts, Rouen, and Grand Palais, Paris 1975, No. 19.

Bibliography: A&P. No. 163; cat. Hotel Drouot, Paris 1967, No. 56.

1. MOMA, 1953, No. 35.
2. RSJ, 1967, No. 43.
3. RSJ, 1975, No. 66.
4. AIC, 1976, No. 30.
5. L&S, 1964, No. 25.
6. LGI, 1970, No. 95.
7. MFAB, 1964, No. 41.
    (full page image, page 19)
8. FAMB, 1976, No. 23.
9. DIA, 1995, No. 2.
10. RSJ, 1980, No. 55, pict. p. 41.
11. RMA, 1984, No. 52.
12. RSJ, 1989B, No. 45, pict. p. 109.
13. RSJ, 1991, No 48, pict. p. 121.
14. RSJ, 2005, No. 40, pict. p. 79.

Technique: hard ground etching and drypoint.

Time: Another of the movement towards Cubist sensibilities, the raised arms seen in the earlier print, "Dans La Foret," the strong hatching and absence of background are his current tendencies. Jane Hancock speaks of Villon's volumetric analysis being carried so far as to distortion of the figure. (FAM, 1976, page 47).

Note: Stanley Johnson told me, when I purchased this print, that it represented Villon's earliest foray into Cubism.

1909 "Nu Debout Bras en l'Aire"

35

Type: Etching and Drypoint
Reference: G&P: E245
Edition/Number: 23 / 20
Size--H, W: 21-1/2 x 16 inches
Framed: Yes
Inventory Number: JCL0674
Provenance: R. S. Johnson International #15462 (1/19/1991)

Standing Nude, Back Turned

G&P, 1979: Etching, signed on the plate. Edition of 15.

Exhibitions: Museum of Modern Art, New York 1953, No. 36; B.N., Paris 1959, No. 51; M.D.C., Le Havre 1962, No. 11; Gallery Louis Square, Paris 1963, No. 4; Museum of Fine Arts, Rouen, and Grand Palais, Paris 1975, No. 20.

Bibliography: A&P. No. 166.

1. MOMA, 1953, No. 36.
2. RSJ, 1975, No. 68.
3. FAM, 1976, No. 24.
4. RSJ, 1989B, No. 46, pict. p. 111.
5. RSJ, 1991, No. 49, pict. p. 123.
6. RSJ, 2005, No. 38, pict. p. 75.

Technique: hard ground etching and drypoint (?).

Time: This is another in the recent (1909) series where Villon begins to simplify, centering the subject, and employs the triangular hatching that is both his natural tendency and which also conforms to his legacy (self-proclaimed) to Leonardo. The use of long hatch lines is a typical Villon technique.

Note: Jane Hancock, FAM, 1976, page 47, comments on this print: the model may have been Renée (the subject of the Minne prints, Leissring, 2011) and also the prints with her name included in the title. Hancock feels the subject is treated with "monumentality," as a sculptural form transmuted to paper."The sharp contrasts of light and dark establish an ample and complex rhythm." Villon's "mature" drawing style may be evidenced here, Ms. Hancock writes, by the encircling of highlights and shading beneath them. RSJ dates this print to 1910.

1909 "Femme Debout De Dos"

Type: Etching (with Drypoint?)
Reference: G&P: E248
Edition/Number: 15 / 8
Size--H, W: 12-1/2 x 7 inches
Framed: Yes
Inventory Number: JCL1145
Provenance: R. S. Johnson International (4/2/1992)

Dance At The Moulin Rouge (first of three prints of this image)

G&P, 1979: Etching.
First state, 39.2 cm x 30 cm, with lines only, before the signature is engraved, a few proofs, of which one is trimmed (38 cm x 29 cm) at the Cabinet des Estampes, B.N.; (See page 40) Second state, 39.2 cm x 30 cm, many shadow works and signature engraved two proofs according to Villon's annotations, the number one, printed as it is, for the other, number two, Villon used the retroussee method (wiped etching) before printing; (see page 40) Third state, the plate is cut horizontally at the level of the orchestra to 23.3 cm x 30cm, two proofs; Fourth state, the plate is cut twice, the vertical cut separates the guard from the rest of the subjects: a few proofs the part (left side) with the guard , 23.3 cm x 9.7 cm, which later had been printed at a bigger number to illustrate a book, the right part is cut again at the top under the orchestra, to 17.2 cm x 20.3, three proofs.

Exhibitions: Museum of Modem Art, New York 1953, No. 37; Gallery Louis Square, Paris 1954, No. 22; Antwerp 1955, No. 173; Oslo 1958, No. 14; B.N. , Paris 1959, No. 52; Stockholm 1960s, No. 108; Galerie Charpentier, Paris 1961, No. 160; Chicago 1967, No. 44.; Museum of Fine Arts, Rouen 1967; Gallery Sagot-Le Garrec, Paris 1975, No. 20. (3rd state).

Bibliography: A&P, 1950 No. 172 ; cat. Hotel Drouot, Paris 1962, No. 22; 1967, No. 59; Pierre Cabanne, Les 3 Duchamp, Neuchatel 1975.

Note: there is confusion in identifying the state of these three images, and even the images referred to by RSJ (twice) and AIC (once). See next and following prints.

1. MOMA, 1953, No. 37.
2. RSJ, 1967, No 44. (This is the 3rd state see page 40)
3. AIC, 1976, No. 34. (states "3rd state of 3" but, see G&P above)
4. RSJ, 1975, No. 69.
5. PMA, 2001, No 2a, 2b.
6. MMS, 1960, No. 108.
7. RSJ, 1980, No. 56, pict. p. 43.
8. RSJ, 1989B, No. 47, pict. p. 113.
9. RSJ, 1991, No. 50, pict. p. 125.

1910 "Bal du Moulin Rouge" (La Garde)

Type: Etching
Reference: G&P: E249 iv/iv
Edition/Number: not stated / proof
Size--H, W: 8-3/4 x 3 inches
Framed: Matted
Inventory Number: JCL0751
Provenance: W. F. Maibaum F. A. (8/17/1991)

Dance At The Moulin Rouge (second of three prints of this image)

Please refer to page 38 for additional information about this print.

This is the first state according to G&P, (see page 38) showing only the lines of the image to come. Notice that the soldier is at the lower left of this image, in outline form.

E 249.   1er état

E 249.   2e état

This image is what G&P have called the second state. This is hard ground etching with the bitten areas showing in very dark contrasts. See page 38 for additional notes on this state.

1910 "Bal du Moulin Rouge" (La Garde)

Type: Etching
Reference: G&P: E249 iv/iv
Edition/Number: not stated / proof
Size--H, W: 8-3/4 x 3 inches
Framed: Matted
Inventory Number: JCL2127
Provenance: Larry Saphire/W. F. Maibaum F. A. (2/23/1994)

Dance At The Moulin Rouge (Third of three prints of this image)

Please refer to page 38 for additional information about this print.

The references are very confusing as to the identification of states. G&P (see page 38) calls this image the 3rd state. The top of the plate of the 2nd state (see image on page 40) has been trimmed. There were very few proofs of this print..

E 249.   3ᵉ état

E 249.   4ᵉ état

This image is what G&P define as the fourth state. It is the right portion of the plate, without the soldier, and trimmed further, to include only the balcony. Thus, if G&P are correct, the three prints in my collection are all 5th or final states.

1910 "Bal du Moulin Rouge" (La Garde)

Type: Etching
Reference: G&P: E249 iv/iv
Edition/Number: not stated / proof
Size--H, W: 8-3/4 x 3 inches
Framed: Matted
Inventory Number: JCL2265
Provenance: Larry Saphire/W. F. Maibaum F. A. (7/25/1994)

Frontal Portrait Of Renée or Portrait Of A Young Woman

G&P, 1979: Etching; Thirty proofs.

Exhibitions: Rath Museum, Geneva 1955, No. 141; French Institute, Athens 1958; B.N. , Paris 1959, No. 55; Gallery Light, New York 1964, No. 27; Chicago 1967, No. 48 ; Gallery L. Goldschmidt, New-York 1970, No. 103; Gallery Sagot-Le Garrec, Paris 1975, No. 23.

Bibliography: A&P, 1950 No. 182 ; cat. Hotel Drouot, Paris 1967, No. 63; Pierre Cabanne, Les 3 Duchamp, Neuchatel 1975.

1. MOMA, 1953, No. 44.
2. RSJ, 1967, No. 48. (Johnson states that this is the smaller of two plates devoted to this subject)
3. MFAB, 1964, No. 45. (larger plate)
4. RSJ, 1975, No. 74 (small plate)
5. L&S, 1964, No. 27. (small plate)
6. AIC, 1976, No. 37. (small plate)
7. FAM, 1976, No. 25. (large plate)
8. PMA, 2001, No. 3. (large plate)
9. RSJ, 1990, No. 26, pict. p. 53.

Technique: hard ground etching.

Time: Jane Hancock, FAM, 1976, page 48, describes the four prints of Renée (the model for the Minne series) as representing "a high point in the sculptural representation of the human figure." Ms. Hancock finds that the graphic studies were preludes to the processes Villon used later in his painting, the development of sculptural masses with volumes based upon graded tones (in the graphics) and by use of Leonardo's pyramids and color choices in the paintings that followed.

Note: This print was preceded by a painting, in reverse direction, and as such is a common way Villon approaches his printmaking—this is not common amongst artists.

1911 "Renée de Face"

45

          Type: Etching
    Reference: G&P: E261
Edition/Number: 30 / 21
   Size--H, W: 11 x 7-1/2 inches
      Framed: Yes
Inventory Number: JCL0671
   Provenance: R. S. Johnson International #15525 (10/25/1990)

Musicians At The Cafe

G&P, 1979: Etching, first worked with thin Varnish and aquatint.
Five working states, of which a few proofs were printed: First state, thin varnish only (the plate looks like a sketch); second state, aquatint is added, one proof is annotated -second state, first grain; third state, some brush bites on the guitarist's and the organist's clothes; fourth state, some works in etching, the guitarist's feet and the bottom of the harp are not finished; fifth state, works on the guitarist's feet and the bottom of the harp, these works hide the signature, we can see some traces of aquatint; final state, the traces of aquatint are wiped: Fifty proofs.

Exhibitions: Museum of Modem Art, New York 1953, No. 39; Gallery L. Goldschmidt, New York 1955, No. 19; Rath Museum, Geneva 1955, No. 143; Museum of Fine Arts, Boston 1964, No. 48; Chicago 1967, No. 49; Gallery G. Cramer, Geneva 1967, No. 12; Gallery L. Goldschmidt, New York 1970, No. 106, No. 107; Gallery Sagot-Le Garrec, Paris 1975, No. 25.

Bibliography: A&P, 1950 No. 185 ; Pierre Cabanne, Les 3 Duchamp, Neuchatel 1975.

1. FAM, 1970, No. 48. (the illustrated image looks like G&P final state)
2. RSJ, 1967, No 49. (image is final state)
3. RSJ, 1975, No. 75. (image is final state)
4. RSJ, 1978, No. 32. (image is final state)
5. MOMA, 1953, No. 39.
6. AIC, 1976, No. 38.
7. PMA, 2001, No. 6. (final state)
8. RMA, 1984, No. 56, pict. p. 56.
9. RSJ, 1989B, No. 48, pict. p. 115.
10. RSJ, 1990, No. 27, pict. p. 55.
11. RSJ, 1991, No. 51, pict. p. 127.
12. RSJ, 2003, No. 35, pict. p. 59.
13. RSJ, 2005, No. 41, pict. p. 81.

Technique: Etching and softening with aquatint.

Time: This is an interesting transition print. The subject carries the memories of the illustrator and of the Belle Epoque influences of Toulouse-Lautrec, especially in this state (as annotated on my print by Villon) but in the final state, as Johnson remarks: An important work in Villon's advance to Cubism" RSJ, 1978, page 36. Villon removes the softness of the early proofs and shows forceful geometry in the final print. The annotation is hard to read:

1912 "Musiciens Chez le Bistro"

Type:	Etching with Aquatint
Reference:	G&P: E270 iii/iv
Edition/Number:	Third State: See page 46, G&P 1979--one of "few proofs"
Size--H, W:	10-1/2 x 9 inches
Framed:	Yes
Inventory Number:	JCL1120
Provenance:	Annex Gallery #TF102 (8/13/1991)

Frontal Portrait Of Yvonne

G&P, 1979: Dry Point.
A few proofs of a state (in one proof, the bottom of the plate is not worked, some proofs before the trimming and before the signature); final state, twenty eight proofs.

Exhibitions: Salon d'Automne, Paris 1913, No. 2074 ; Gallery Louis Square, Paris 1954, No. 26; Antwerp 1955, No. 177; Rath Museum, Geneva 1955, No. 149; Gallery Louis Square, Paris 1957, No. 3; Oslo 1958, No. 18; French Institute, Athens 1958; B.N. , Paris 1959, No. 60; Gallery Louis Square, Paris 1963, No. II; Gallery Light, New York 1964, No. 34; Chicago 1967, No. 54; Museum of Fine Arts, Rouen 1967; Gallery Sagot-Le Garrec, Paris 1975, No. 30.

Bibliography: A&P, 1950 No. 195; cat. Hotel Drouot, Paris 1962, No. 24; Pierre Cabanne, Les 3 Duchamp, Neuchatel 1975.

1. L&S, 1964, No. 34.
2. RSJ, 1967, No. 54.
3. RSJ, 1975, No. 84.
4. AIC, 1976, No. 48.
5. PMA, 2001, No.. 12.
6. MMS, 1960, No. 110.
7. RSJ, 1976, No. 87, pict. p. 50.
8. RSJ, 1989B, No. 52, pict. p. 123.
9. RSJ, 1990, No. 28, pict. p. 57.
10. RSJ, 1991, No. 55, pict. p. 135.
11. PMA, 2001, No. 12, pict. p. 26.
12. RSJ, 2001, No. 11, pict. p. 27.
13. RSJ, 2003, No. 38, pict. p. 63.
14. RSJ, 2005, No. 43, pict. p. 85.

Technique: Drypoint.

Time: Innis Howe Shoemaker makes reference to Villon's influence by da Vinci's Trattato della pittura, wherein Leonardo asserts that all forms can be distilled into what he called pyramidal shapes but which on the flat plane are really triangles. Ms Shoemaker feels that in this portrait of his sister, Villon used "the most radical application of pyramidal construction." Villon's use of the long hatch line and his deep invasion of the surface of the plate are well demonstrated, as is his contrasting areas of high light, subtended by deep shadow. Villon pulled 28 prints from this plate.

Note: This is one of my favorite prints. I can feel the influence of Cubism and the intelligence that Cubist theory imposed upon the artist who embraced its potentials. The model is Villon's sister, Yvonne.

1913 "Yvonne D. de Face"

Type: Drypoint
Reference: G&P:E281; A&P: 195
Edition/Number: 28 / 19
Size--H, W: 21-1/2 x 16 inches
Framed: Yes
Inventory Number: JCL0710
Provenance: W. F. Maibaum F. A. (3/18/1991)

The Little Tightrope Walker (Équilibriste)

G&P, 1979: Dry Point, signed and dated on the plate.
Fifty proofs, then in 1955, another printing to illustrate J. Lassaigne's book, Eulogy of Jacques Villon, cf. E 544 and E 547. Same subject as the engraving E 286, but treated more freely. Realized from a 1913 painting, copied in, Jacques Villon, by Dora Vallier, p. 48.

Exhibitions: Museum of Modem Art, New York 1953, No. 48; Gallery Louis Square, Paris 1954, No. 30; Antwerp 1955, No. 181; Rath Museum, Geneva 1955, No. 150; Gallery L. Goldschmidt, New York 1955, No. 24; Oslo 1958, No. 22; French Institute, Athens 1958; B.N.., Paris 1959, No. 65; Galerie Charpentier, Paris 1961, No. 164; M.D.C., Le Havre 1962, No. 19; Gallery Light, New York 1964, No. 38; Museum of Fine Arts, Boston 1964, No. 57; Chicago 1967, No. 60; Gallery G. Cramer, Geneva 1967, No. 15; Museum of Fine Arts, Rouen 1967; Gallery Sagot-Le Garrec, Paris 1975, No. 34; Museum of Fine Arts, Rouen, and Grand Palais, Paris 1975, No. 56.

Bibliography: A&P, 1950, 1950 No. 201; Graphis, No. 53.

1. L&S, 1964, No. 38.
2. MFAB, 1964.
3. RSJ, 1967, No. 60.
4. RSJ, 1975, No. 90.
5. FAM, 1976, No. 57.
6. PMA, 2001, No. 18a, b, pict. p. 43.
7. RSJ, 1989A, No. 10, pict. p. 25.
8. RSJ, 1989B, No. 58, pict. p. 135.
9. RSJ, 1991, No. 61, pict. p. 147.

Technique: Drypoint.

Time: In the years 1913 and 1914, Villon made drawings of an acrobat, in several degrees of abstraction, attempting to find the movements of the tight-rope walker in a single drawing, and later, plate. Movement is implied by the use of organic lines (swirls) in association with geometric, triangular and pyramidal forms. The love he had for the long parallel hatch lines which cover the entire plate and which somehow soften the image without addition of aquatint or soft ground is evidenced here. This is another of my favorite prints. There are three versions of this print in the collection. The two following are from the 1955 printing. This one is pencil signed, LR.

1914 "Le Petit Équilibriste"

Type: Drypoint
Reference: G&P: E286
Edition/Number: 50 / 6
Size--H, W: 8-5/8 x 6 inches
Framed: Yes
Inventory Number: JCL2070
Provenance: R. S. Johnson International, #15390 (3/22/1990)

The Little Tightrope Walker (Équilibriste)

G&P, 1979: Dry Point, signed and dated on the plate.
Fifty proofs- then in 1955, another printing to illustrate J. Lassaigne's book, Eulogy of Jacques Villon, cf. E 544 and E 547. Same subject as the engraving E 286, but treated more freely. Realized from a 1913 painting, copied in, Jacques Villon, by Dora Vallier, p. 48.

Exhibitions: Museum of Modern Art, New York 1953, No. 48; Gallery Louis Square, Paris 1954, No. 30; Antwerp 1955, No. 181; Rath Museum, Geneva 1955, No. 150; Gallery L. Goldschmidt, New York 1955, No. 24; Oslo 1958, No. 22; French Institute, Athens 1958; B.N..., Paris 1959, No. 65; galerie Charpentier, Paris 1961, No. 164; M. D. C., Le Havre 1962, No. 19; Gallery Light, New York 1964, No. 38; Museum of Fine Arts, Boston 1964, No. 57; Chicago 1967, No. 60; Gallery G. Cramer, Geneva 1967, No. 15; Museum of Fine Arts, Rouen 1967; Gallery Sagot-Le Garrec, Paris 1975, No. 34; Museum of Fine Arts, Rouen, and Grand Palais, Paris 1975, No. 56.

Bibliography: A&P, 1950, 1950 No. 201; Graphis, No. 53

1. L&S, 1964, No. 38.
2. MFAB, 1964.
3. RSJ, 1967, No. 60.
4. RSJ, 1975, No. 90.
5. FAM, 1976, No. 57.
6. PMA, 2001, No. 18a, b, pict. p. 43.
7. RSJ, 1989A, No. 10, pict. p. 25.
8. RSJ, 1989B, No. 58, pict. p. 135.
9. RSJ, 1991, No. 61, pict. p. 147.

Technique: Drypoint.
Time: In the years 1913 and 1914, Villon made drawings of an acrobat, in a several degrees of abstraction, attempting to find the movements of the tight-rope walker in a single drawing, and later, plate. Movement is implied by the use of organic lines (swirls) in association with geometric, triangular and pyramidal forms. The love he had for the long parallel hatch lines which cover the entire plate and which somehow soften the image without addition of aquatint or soft ground is evidenced here. This is another of my favorite prints in the collection. There are three versions of this print in the collection. This print is from the 1955 printing. It is pencil signed, LR and signed and dated on the plate.

Jacques Villon. L'équilibre. Huile sur toile. 1913.

1914 "Le Petit Équilibriste" 1955 print

Type: Drypoint
Reference: G&P: E286 (S)--1955 printing
Edition/Number: 50 / 6
Size--H, W: 8-5/8 x 6 inches
Framed: Matted
Inventory Number: JCL1729
Provenance: W. F. Maibaum Fine Art (6/11/1991)

The Little Tightrope Walker (Équilibriste)

G&P, 1979: Dry Point, signed and dated on the plate.
Fifty proofs- then in 1955, another printing to illustrate J. Lassaigne's book, Eulogy of Jacques Villon, cf. E 544 and E 547. Same subject as the engraving E 286, but treated more freely. Realized from a 1913 painting, copied in, Jacques Villon, by Dora Vallier, p. 48.

Exhibitions: Museum of Modem Art, New York 1953, No. 48; Gallery Louis Square, Paris 1954, No. 30; Antwerp 1955, No. 181 ; Rath Museum, Geneva 1955, No. 150; Gallery L. Goldschmidt, New York 1955, No. 24; Oslo 1958, No. 22; French Institute, Athens 1958; B.N..., Paris 1959, No. 65; galerie Charpentier, Paris 1961, No. 164; M.D.C., Le Havre 1962, No. 19; Gallery Light, New York 1964, No. 38; Museum of Fine Arts, Boston 1964, No. 57; Chicago 1967, No. 60; Gallery G. Cramer, Geneva 1967, No. 15; Museum of Fine Arts, Rouen 1967; Gallery Sagot-Le Garrec, Paris 1975, No. 34; Museum of Fine Arts, Rouen, and Grand Palais, Paris 1975, No. 56.

Bibliography: A&P, 1950, 1950 No. 201; Graphis, No. 53.

1. L&S, 1964, No. 38.
2. MFAB, 1964.
3. RSJ, 1967, No. 60.
4. RSJ, 1975, No. 90.
5. FAM, 1976, No. 57.
6. PMA, 2001, No. 18a, b, pict. p. 43.
7. RSJ, 1989A, No. 10, pict. p. 25.
8. RSJ, 1989B, No. 58, pict. p. 135.
9. RSJ, 1991, No. 61, pict. p. 147.

Technique: Drypoint.

Time: In the years 1913 and 1914, Villon made drawings of an acrobat, in a several degrees of abstraction, attempting to find the movements of the tight-rope walker in a single drawing, and later, plate. Movement is implied by the use of organic lines (swirls) in association with geometric, triangular and pyramidal forms. The love he had for the long parallel hatch lines which cover the entire plate and which somehow soften the image without addition of aquatint or soft ground is evidenced here. This is another of my favorite prints in the collection. There are three versions of this print in the collection. This unsigned print is from the 1955 printing of the 1914 plate (plate signed and dated). Finally, there is another numbered edition of this print, in a series of 200 of which the collection owns number 103.

1914 "Le Petit Équilibriste" 1955 print

Type: Drypoint
Reference: G&P: E286 (U) 1955 printing
Edition/Number: 50 / not numbered
Size--H, W: 8-5/8 x 6 inches
Framed: Matted
Inventory Number: JCL0730
Provenance: W. F. Maibaum Fine Art (6/11/1991)

Baudelaire (With Pedestal)

G&P, 1979: Etching.
First state, some proofs; second state, new work, some trial proofs before the signature; final state, signature engraved, fifty proofs.

Engraved from a 1911 Duchamp-Villon sculpture. This bust of Baudelaire played an important role in Villon's work. In the Puteaux workshop, the sculpture was often the topic of discussion. "If the air pressure in the room was suddenly removed, we imagined that these objects would explode in a manner defined by the pressure inside the lines of force."(V)

Exhibitions: International Exhibition of 1937, Paris, "Etching and Engraving," No. 330; Gallery Louis Square, Paris 1954, No. 33; Antwerp 1955, No. 184; Gallery L. Goldschmidt, New York 1955, No. 26; Rath Museum, Geneva 1955, No. 152; Oslo 1958, No. 25; B.N..., Paris 1959, No. 68; Stockholm 1960s, No. 113; galerie Charpentier Paris 1961, No. 167; M.D.C. , Le Havre 1962, No. 21; Gallery Light, New York 1964, No. 39; Museum of Fine Arts, Boston 1964, No. 60; Chicago 1967, No. 63; Museum of Fine Arts, Rouen 1967; Gallery G. Cramer, Geneva 1967, No. 17; Gallery Sagot-Le Garrec, Paris 1975, No. 37; Museum of Fine Arts, Rouen, and Grand Palais, Paris 1975, No. 69.

Bibliography: A&P. No. 204 repr.

1. MOMA, 1953, No. 51.
2. MMS, 1960, No. 113.
3. L&S, 1964, No. 39.
4. MFAB, 1964, No. 60, pict. p. 50.
5. RSJ, 1967, No. 63, pict. p. 40.
6. RSJ, 1975, No. 93, pict. p. 48.
7. AIC, 1976, No. 57, pict. p. 24.
8. FAM, 1976, No. 71, pict. p. 94.
9. RMA, 1984, No. 62, iii/iii, pict. p. 62.
10. DIA, 1995, No. 1, pict. p. 2.
11. RSJ, 2005, No. 47, pict. p. 93.
12. PMA, 2001, No. 21, pict. p. 49.

Technique: Hard ground etching.

Time: Raymond Duchamp-Villon died in 1918. Villon began making studies of his brother's powerful sculpture of 1911. There are several photographs of drawings and paintings made by Villon in advance of the etching shown in the FAM, 1976 catalog (pages 91-95).

Note: David Rubin describes (FAM, 1976-page 94) Villon's personal fondness for this etching, for he included its final version in the series of aquatints made for Bernheim-Jeune between 1922 and 1930.

1920 "Baudelaire (Au Socle)"

Type:	Etching
Reference:	G&P: E290 iii/iii
Edition/Number:	50 / AP (artist's proof)
Size--H, W:	16-3/8 x 11 inches
Framed:	Yes
Inventory Number:	JCL0675
Provenance:	Annex Gallery #REL:101 (7/23/1990)

Baudelaire (Without Base)

G&P, 1979: Etching.
Engraved for Architecture, a public collection under the direction of Andre Mare and Louis Süe (see E 600 and E 632--G&P, 1979); a proof before steeling and six proofs pulled aside.

Exhibitions: Museum of Modern Art, New York 1953, No. 52 reproduced full-page frontispiece.

Bibliography: A&P No. 466.

1. MOMA, 1953, No. 52
2. PMA, 2001, No. 22, pict. p. 50

Technique: Hard Ground etching.

Time: 1920, after Villon's brother's death (1918). Villon kept a plaster of this sculpture in his studio at Puteaux. He produced three paintings, a gouache and eight drawings to the study of this piece, in addition to the two etchings. The present study is without the pedestal (socle) and is done using only precise horizontal lines of slightly variable width (to generate the shadows). In the studies devoted to the first engraving (page 57) Villon believed that he had expressed, using only parallel hatching, the entire science of engraving (PMA, 2001, page 48).

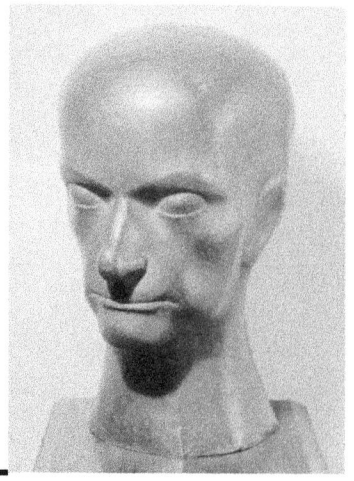

Raymond Duchamp-Villon,
Bronze, 1911

J. Villon, Buadelaire, 1920,
Drawing

J. Villon, Buadelaire,
1920, Watercolor

1920 "Baudelaire (Sans Le Socle)"

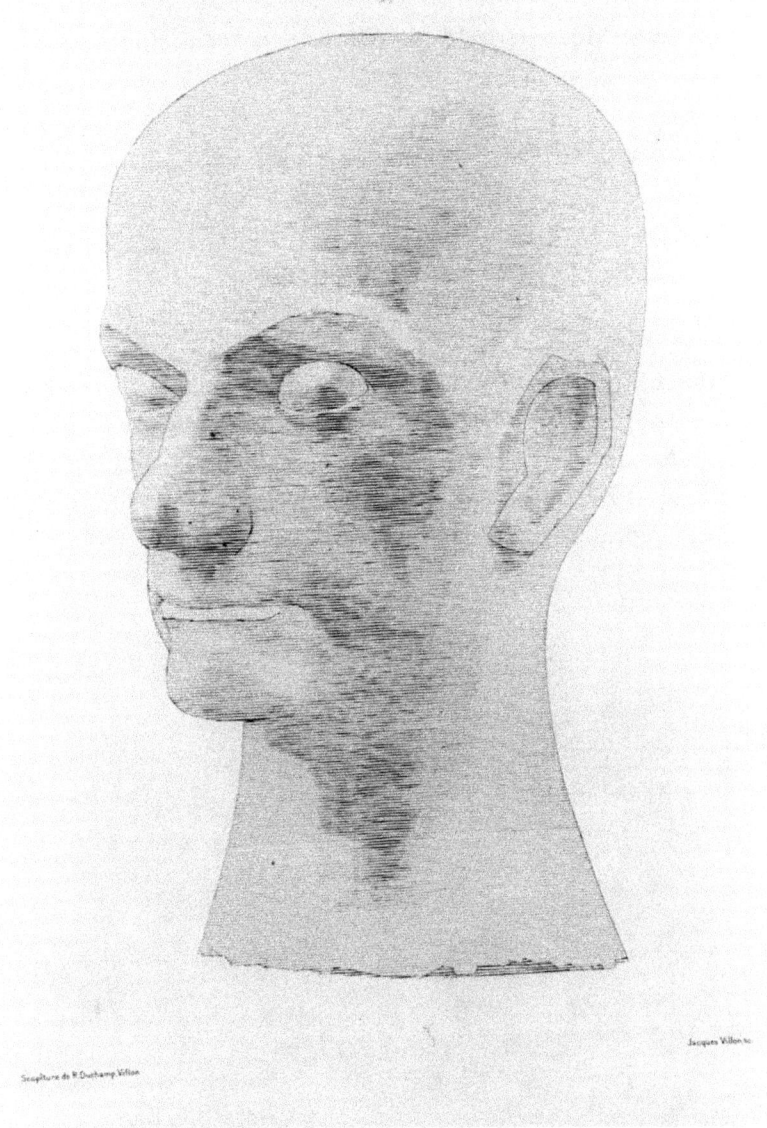

Type: Etching
Reference: G&P: E291 (US)
Edition/Number: not stated / unnumbered
Size--H, W: 13-1/8 x 7 inches
Framed: Matted
Inventory Number: JCL0736
Provenance: W. F. Maibaum F. A. (6/11/1991)

Baudelaire (Without Base)

G&P, 1979: Etching.
Engraved for Architecture, a public collection under the direction of Andre Mare and Louis Süe (see E 600 and E 632--G&P, 1979); a proof before steeling and six proofs pulled aside.

Exhibitions: Museum of Modern Art, New York 1953, No. 52 reproduced full-page frontispiece.

Bibliography: A&P No. 466.

1. MOMA, 1953, No.52.
2. PMA, 2001, No. 22, pict. p. 50.

Notes: See the two previous etchings. As the studies of the bust of Baudelaire progress, one can see the methods Villon employed using the theories developed after the war, especially in the studies devoted to the *Table d'echecs* (page 63). This can be seen best in the gouache entitled *"Un Buste,"* 1920, below. One can come to understand the devotion Villon had to technical and theoretical precision in the development of his subjects. Also see *"Cheval,"* next.

J. Villon, Study for a Baudelaire, 1921, Drawing

J. Villon, "Un Buste," Gouache, 1920

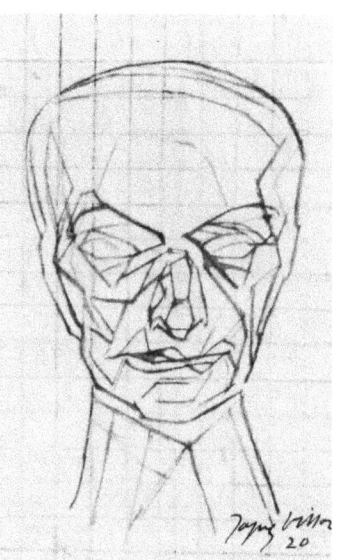

J. Villon, Charles Baudelaire, 1920, Drawing

1920 "Baudelaire (Sans Le Socle)"

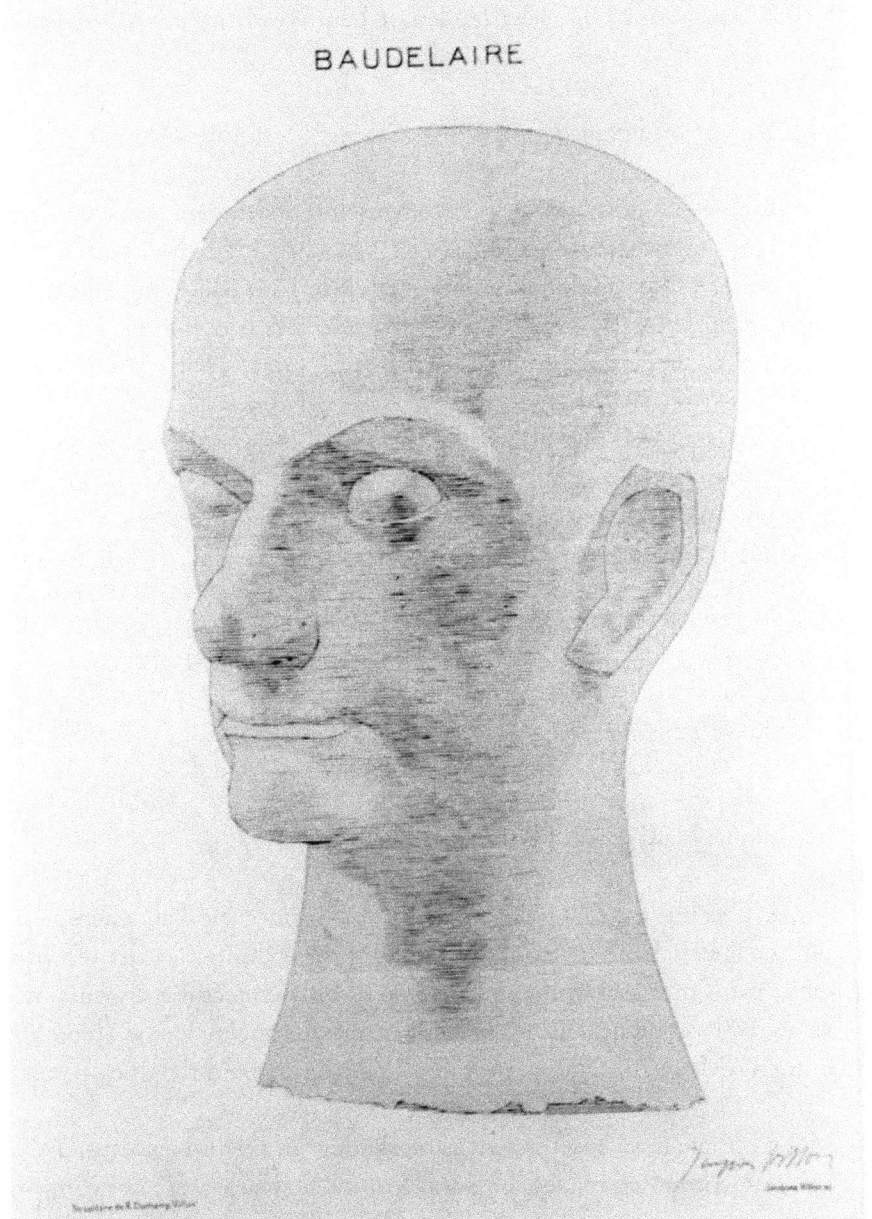

Type:	Etching
Reference:	G&P: E291 (S) signed LR
Edition/Number:	not stated / unnumbered
Size--H, W:	13-1/8 x 7 inches
Framed:	Matted
Inventory Number:	JCL0737
Provenance:	W. F. Maibaum F. A. (6/11/1991)

Table d'echecs or Game of Chess

G&P: A few trial proofs, then, after cleaning the Bevels, printed in an edition of 125 for the German magazine DIE Schaffenden of Paul Westheim published by Gustav Kiepenheuer in Potsdam.

Cf. : Repeat of a painting of 1919, "Game" (coll. Louis Carré).

Exhibitions: La Sectiond'Or, 1925; Museum of Modem Art, New York 1953, No. 50; Gallery Louis Square, Paris 1954, No. 32; Antwerp 1955, No. 183; Oslo 1958, No. 24; B.N..., Paris 1959, No. 67; Stockholm 1960s, No. 114; Museum of Fine Arts, Boston 1964, No. 59; Lisbon 1966, No. 7; Chicago 1967, No. 62; Museum of Fine Arts, Rouen, and Grand Palais, Paris 1975, No. 65; Gallery Sagot-Le Garrec, Paris 1975, No. 36.

Bibliography: A&P No. 203 harp.; cat. Hotel Drouot, Paris 1962, No. 27, 1967, No. 69.

1. MOMA, 1953, No. 50.
2. MMS, 1960, No. 114.
3. RSJ, 1967, No 62, pict. p. 40.
4. RSJ, 1975, No. 92, pict. p. 48.
5. AIC, 1976, No. 56. (annotated)
6. FAM, 1976, No. 69a, pict. p. 91.
7. RSJ, 1978, No. 39, pict. cover. (annotated)
8. RSJ, 1980, No. 62, pict. p. 47.
9. RSJ, 1989B, No. 60, pict. pp. 138, 139.
10. RSJ, 1991, No. 63, pict. pp. 150, 151.
11. RSJ, 1999A, No. 45, pict. p. 85.
12. RSJ, 1999B, No. 31, pict. p. 57.
13. PMA, 2001, No. 20, pict. p. 47.
13. RSJ, 2001, No. 13, pict. p. 31.
14. RSJ, 2003, No. 39, pict. p. 65. (annotated)
15. RSJ, 2005, No. 46, ii/ii, pict. p. 91.

Technique: Hard ground etching.

Time: This was the first print made by Villon since the war, where he was attached to a camouflage unit in Eu. The painting (Jeu) and the etching were derived from a study of a chess table, made into a drawing, in the form of an architectural drawing, with elevation and "plan" views. By structurally tilting the table at various angles, a new object emerges. This is discussed in the FAM, 1976, catalog, page 89. The painting and the drawing are pictured.

Note: His analysis, based on areas of shadow and light have caused Villon to break his subject into superimposed planes: This was Villon's first post war engraving--he went from analysis to synthesis. The study of planes was based on a system of measurements, with the object central but embodied in space, which was itself changed in relation to the object--the object, a chess board is seen in dual perspective inside a pyramidal construction, whose superimposed places serve to some extent as the object's foundation. This sober, powerfully structured art is justified by scientific knowledge of the object's shape, volume, position and development in space.

1920 "Table D'Echecs"

Type: Etching
Reference: G&P: E292
Edition/Number: 125 / unnumbered, pencil signed LR
Size--H, W: 8 x 6 inches
Framed: Yes
Inventory Number: JCL0654
Provenance: R. S. Johnson International #15079 (4/24/1989)

Gallop or The Horse

G&P, 1979: Etching, signed on the plate
Edition of 50, and in 1947 signed edition of 50, including 35 accompanying the deluxe copies of *Du Cubism* by Albert Gleizes and Jean Metzinger (20 of these copies are also accompanied by a proof in sanguine, unsigned); In addition, there were 400 black prints, unsigned, to accompany the regular copies of the book (some of these proofs were subsequently signed by the artist).

"Following numerous sketches the horse has been divided into parts, the top through a series of profiles that limit the various planes of its thickness. These planes are folded but many are deleted."(V.).

This is part of a series on the decomposition of movement. Villon is in his abstract period, but remains by his starting point in the game of chess. "I adhere to the spirit of Cubism but not its rigidity, total abstract is not for me, I like life too much."

Exhibitions: Galerie Louis Carré, Paris 1954, No. 34; Rath Museum, Geneva 1955, No. 153, Antwerp 1955, No. 185, Oslo 1958, No. 27 repr., BN, Paris 1959, No. 71, repr., Galerie Charpentier, Paris 1961, No. 169; MDC, The Harbour 1962, No. 23; Light Gallery, New York 1964, No. 41, Museum of Fine Arts, Boston 1964, No. 61 repr., Chicago, 1967, No. 65; Gallery G. Cramer, Geneva 1967, No. 18. Museum of Fine Arts, Rouen, 1967; Sagot-Le Garrec Gallery, Paris 1975, No. 39 repr.

Bibliography: A&P No. 206. (repr. in reverse)
1. L&S, 1964, No. 41.
2. MFAB, 1964, NO. 61, pict. p. 51.
3. RSJ, 1967, No. 65, pict. p. 45.
4. RSJ, 1975, No. 95, pict. p. 49.

Technique: Hard ground etching.

Time: Following the experiments of the Table d'echecs, Villon began to refine his method of showing objects as superimposed planes or layers. Also see following image, a reproduction in color aquatint of George Braque's "Nature Morte," which shows the picture plane flattening of the "so called" Cubists and Villon's experiments in layering. It should be emphasized that Villon is asking the viewer to participate in the experiment, so important to his method, where what is to be demonstrated is not directly revealed and demands that the viewer use his own intellect to discover the picture;s meaning or intent. See Dora Vallier's comment, page 15,: "Villon's art does not yield to the eyes unless it is first approached by the mind."

1921 "Le Cheval"

Type: Etching, plate signed, pencil signed LR, annotated LL
Reference: G&P: E295
Edition/Number: 50 / unnumbered
Size--H, W: 3-1/16 x 5 inches
Framed: Matted
Inventory Number: JCL1725
Provenance: John Storks/Annex Gallery #TF105 (2/28/1992)

Braque, Nature Morte

G&P: Aquatint, 58.9 x 21.7 cm. 21 proofs in black and 200 color proofs, signed and justified, edited by Bernhcim-Jeunc, and printed by Chalcographie du Louvre, not signed.

Exhibitions: Gallery Bernhcim-Jeunc, Paris 1928; Rath Museum, Geneva 1955, No. 269; Light Gallery, New York 1964, our 94 and 95.

Bibliography: A&P No. 503; cat. Hotel Drouot, Paris 1962, No. 85.

L&S, 1964, No. 95.
AIC, 1976, No. 113.

Technique: Aquatint; a "reproduction in aquatint" of Braque's still life painting.

Time: Between 1922 and 1930, Villon was induced to make a large series of aquatint plates after the paintings of well known fellow artists. Francis Steegmuller, in 1954, took his typewriter to Villon's studio at Puteaux. Villon dictated historical records of his life "in the third person."

"By 1920 pressing financial need obliged JV to turn once again to etching. It was then that he made about forty color aquatints, of rather large format, after paintings by his fellow-artists, Picasso, Matisse, etc. At this time he also etched plates for a book on architecture.

Because of all these types of work--newspaper drawings, color aquatints, reproductions--JV unquestionably found himself, as a painter, twenty-five to thirty years behind his fellow-artists. Some of the latter still tend to look upon him, somewhat dogmatically, as a print maker, and even as a "graveur-ouvrier" a fact that he had never fully appreciated until very recently. Apparently one must live a long time before one can assert oneself fully! But let us not feel sorry for JV: all has turned out for the best, and his prints live in happy intelligence with his paintings."[38]

This image is included so as to illustrate the relationship between what historians are calling Villon's Cubist prints and the images of George Braque, whose experiments in flattening the picture plane led to the application of the term "Cubist" to his work. (See page 9)

1922 "Braque: Nature Morte"

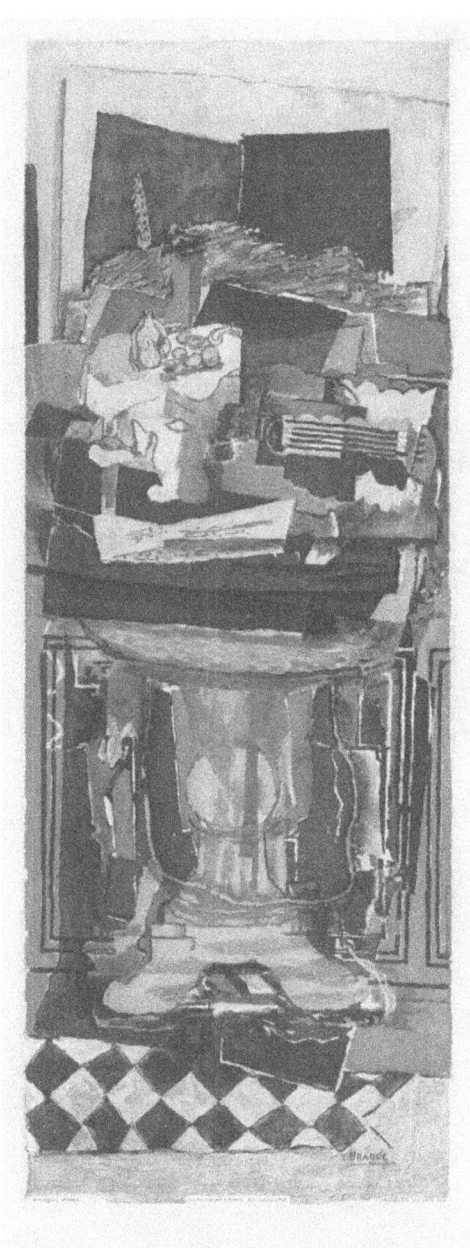

Type: Aquatint
Reference: G&P: E636
Edition/Number: 200 / unnumbered
Size--H, W: 23 x 8-1/2 inches
Framed: Matted
Inventory Number: JCL1285
Provenance: Annex Gallery #11115 (7/8/1992)

Portrait D.

G&P: Etching, 14,1 x 11 cm; signed and dated on the plate, fifty proofs.

Exhibitions: Musée Rath, Genève 1955, No. 157; B.N..., Paris 1959, No. 75; M.D.C., Le Havre 1962, No. 26.

Bibliography: A&P. No. 211 repr.

Technique: Hard ground etching.

Time: Villon at this time was experimenting with long, often parallel hatch lines, pyramidal shapes, deep shadows, and Cubist theories. The resemblance to Duchamp the elder is suggested, although the subject is not otherwise identified.

1926 "Portrait D"

Type: Etching
Reference: G&P: E296
Edition/Number: 50 / 37
Size--H, W: 5-1/2 x 4 inches
Framed: Matted
Inventory Number: JCL1127
Provenance: Annex Gallery (4/17/1992)

Villon, Composition (version)

G&P: Aquatint, 50 X 34,3 cm.
200 proofs in color, signed and justified, edited by Bernhein-Jeune and printed by Chalcographie du Louvre, not signed.

Exhibitions: Museum of Modem Art, New York 1953, No. 55; Musée Rath, Genève 1955, No. 276; Anvers 1955, No. 187; Oslo 1958, No. 28; Museum of Fine Arts, Boston 1964, No. 66.

Bibliographie: A&P. No. 526 repr.; cat. Hôtel Drouot, Paris 1962, No. 94, 1967, No. 118.

L&S, 1964, No. 99.
AIC, 1976, No 116.
DIA, 1995, No. 7. (Incorrectly dated, 1927)

Technique: This version appears to be a photo offset lithograph of the aquatint, possibly given as a Christmas present. This version is signed and pencil annotated "Christmas", bottom right corner. Date is approximate. The aquatint is the only one of Villon's "reproductive" engravings based upon one of his own paintings. (AIC, 1976) For the purposes of this book, the planar relationships show Villon's working method.

1928 "Christmas" related to "Composition"

Type:	Possible photo offset, annotated pencil (Christmas), signed LR
Reference:	G&P: E660 (related)
Edition/Number:	Unknown
Size--H, W:	5 x 3-1/2 inches
Framed:	Matted
Inventory Number:	JCL0693
Provenance:	Annex Gallery, #10614 (12/8/1990)

Children With an Apple

G&P: Etching
First state, dry point, a few proofs; final state, etching, signature and date engraved, fifty proofs.

Exhibitions: Museum of Modem Art, New York 1953, No. 60; Musée Rath, Genève 1955, No. 164; galerie Louis Carré, Paris 1957, No. 12; Oslo 1958, No. 53; galerie Louis Carré, Paris 1963, No. 16.

Bibliographie: A&P. No. 221 repr.; cat. Hôtel Drouot, Paris 1967, No. 75.

MOMA, 1953, No. 60.

Technique: Hard ground etching, second state.

Time: Villon employs Cubist and "da Vinci" theories, using Leonardo's pyramids and hatching to display depth. This print is the second state of two. The first state is shown here:

E 327. 1er état

1929 "Enfants a la Pomme"

Type:	Etching
Reference:	G&P: E327
Edition/Number:	50 / 20
Size--H, W:	7-1/16 x 5 inches
Framed:	Matted
Inventory Number:	JCL2140
Provenance:	Annex Gallery #11618 (2/14/1994)

The Philosopher

G&P: Dry Point and Etching.
First state, dry point, a few proofs; second state, etching, signature and date engraved, a few proofs; final state, deeper biting in some areas, trimming with dry point, fifty proofs.

Exhibitions: Painters, Printmakers, Paris 1933; International Exhibition, Paris 1937 "Etching and Engraving"; "The Young Contemporary Engravers,"London 1946; Museum of Modem Art, New York 1953, No. 63 ; Rath Museum, Geneva 1955, No. 168; Antwerp 1955, No. 192 Harp.; B.N... , Paris 1959, No. 89; Gallery Louis Square, Paris 1954, No. 41; 1957, No. 15; 1963, No. 18; M.D.C., Le Havre 1962, No. 31; Gallery New Boom, Paris 1966; Gallery G. Cramer, Geneva 1967, No. 28.

Bibliography: A&P. No. 226 repr.; cat. Hotel Drouot, Paris 1962, No. 33, 1967, No. 78.

1. MOMA, 1953, No. 63.
2. FAM, 1976, No. 105.
3. AIC, 1976, No. 68, 69.

Technique: Drypoint with etching; the hatching with long lines intersecting in a rectilinear fashion is a typical method used by Villon.

Time: David Rubin in the Fogg museum catalog (p. 122) suggests that while Villon was busy with his series of reproductions, he took time to do individual etchings and paintings based upon sketches made earlier. This work is based upon drawings and oil studies of a male bather reading a newspaper. To Villon the pose suggested a classical pose. True to the Duchamp and Villon tradition, he used inexact titles, seducing the viewer into other interpretations. There is a figure in a later etching, from 1938, that resembles the subject of the present work. Rosen also suggests that portraits of Marcel Duchamp by Villon bore the title : Un Philosophe (A Philosopher).

1930 "Le Philosophe"

Type:	Etching and Dry Point, signed and annotated
Reference:	G&P: E330 iii/iii
Edition/Number:	50 / 14
Size--H, W:	8-7/16 x 6 inches
Framed:	Matted
Inventory Number:	JCL2946
Provenance:	Annex Gallery (3/1/1996)

Mr. Patrelle

G&P: Dry Point and Etching

First state, dry point, twenty proofs; second state, reworked with etching, signature and date engraved, twenty proofs; final state, new works emphasizing the shadowed areas, fifty proofs.

The model is Mr. Patrelle; Villon had made his acquaintance during one of his military service periods.

Exhibitions: Painters, Engravers, Paris 1932, Musée Rath, Geneva 1955, No. 179; BN, Paris 1959, No. 96, Gallery Carré, Paris 1963, No. 22; Light Gallery, New York 1964, No. 62.

Bibliography: A&P. No. 242 repr.

1. L&S, 1964, No. 62.
2. RMA, 1984, No. 68.

Technique: Dry point and etching.

Time: Villon had met Patrelle during military service and did several portraits. The second state (below) shows less emphasis upon the shadows. An earlier likeness of Patrelle (1931) is included in the Cubist work catalog from the Philadelphia Museum of Art, number 27.

E 356.   2ᵉ état

1932 "Monsieur Patrelle"

Type:	Etching and Dry Point, signed LR
Reference:	G&P: E 356 iii/iii
Edition/Number:	50 / 2
Size--H, W:	7-1/8 x 5 inches
Framed:	Matted
Inventory Number:	JCL2945
Provenance:	Annex Gallery (3/1/1996)

From Where One Turns His Back To Life

G&P: Drypoint and etching, 22.1 x 27.5 cm.
First state, drypoint, few prints; final state, hard ground etching added, signature and date engraved 40 prints.

Exhibitions: Painters, Engravers, 1940; Louis Carré Gallery, Paris 1954, No. 50 repr.; Rath Museum, Geneva 1955, No. 212, Antwerp 1955, No. 201 repr., Oslo 1958, No. 41; BN, Paris 1959, No. 114, Stockholm 1960 No. 135; Louis Carré Gallery, Paris 1963, No. 28, Museum of Fine Arts, Boston 1964, No. 96, New Rise Gallery, Paris 1966, Museum of Fine Arts, Rouen 1967.

Bibliography: A&P No. 327, repr.; cat. Hotel Drouot, Paris 1962, No. 63, 1967, No. 90 repr.

Technique: Drypoint (first state) followed by hard ground etching.

Comment: this is inspired by one of Mallarmé's poems: "Fenetres," It is based upon a painting done in 1938. As is Villon's usual technique, the etching is the reverse of the painting. Drypoint first outlines the subject, etching defines the shadows. I have two of these images in the collection. A proof copy (unsigned) is from Raymond Haasen, son of Paul Haasen, Villon's printer (Larry Saphire via W. F. Maibaum).

E 444.   1ᵉʳ état

1939 "D'Ou L'On Tourne L'Epaule a la Vie"

- Type: Drypoint with Etching
- Reference: G&P: E444 ii/ii
- Edition/Number: 40 / 30 and 1 proof (see comment opposite)
- Size--H, W: 8-1/2 x 10 inches
- Framed: Matted
- Inventory Number: JCL0750 and JCL2284
- Provenance: R. E. Lewis #25327 (8/16/1994) W. F. Maibaum (8/14/91)

The Fight

G&P: Etching, 28.1 x 24.9 cm.
First state, drypoint, a few trial proofs, final state, with etching, engraved signature and date, 50 trials and 10 artist's proofs.

Note: In 1939, Villon made several paintings on this theme: The Wrestlers, The Fight, Chaos.

Exhibitions: Painters, Engravers, 1940; Galerie Louis Carré, Paris 1954, 11, No. 52 repr., 1957, No. 29, Antwerp 1955, No. 203, Oslo 1958, No. 43, Institute French, Athens 1958, BN, Paris 1959, No. 116 repr., Stockholm 1960, No. 138 repr., Galerie Charpentier, Paris 1961, No. 182, Galerie Louis Carré, Paris 1963, No. 39, Light Gallery, New York 1964, No. 81, Museum of Fine Arts, Boston 1964, No. 98 repr., Lisbon 1966, No. 15, Museum of Beaux-Arts, Rouen, 1967; Sagot-Le Garrec Gallery, Paris 1975, No. 52 repr.; Museum of Fine Arts, Rouen, and Grand Palais, Paris 1975, No. 124 repr.

Bibliography: A&P No. 329 repr.; cat. Hotel Drouot, Paris 1962, No. 65 repr.

1. MMS, 1960, No. 138.
2. L&S, 1964, No. 81.
3. MFAB, 1964, No. 98, pictured on page 83.
4. FAM, 1976, No. 129, pictured on page 150.
5. RSJ, 1976, No. 90, pictured on page 52.
6. RSJ, 1978, No. 46.
7. RMA, 1984, No. 76, pictured page 78.
8. RSJ, 1989A, No. 11, page 27.

Technique: Drypoint followed by hard ground etching, two states.

Comment: The theme of sport first noted in the book of poetry and etchings (page 224 and page 254-Leissring, 2011) carried forth the technique of movement captured by linear analysis. Initial drawing is in drypoint (right) with the final print employing hard ground etching.

E 445. 1er état

1939 "La Lutte"

Type:	Dry Point and Etching
Reference:	G&P: E445 ii/ii
Edition/Number:	50 / 27
Size--H, W:	11 x 9-3/4 inches
Framed:	Matted
Inventory Number:	JCL2282
Provenance:	R. E. Lewis #25326 (8/16/1994)

Young Woman

G&P: Drypoint and engraving, 28.3 x 20.8 cm.
First state, drypoint, a few trial proofs;, final 40 prints

Exhibitions: Galerie Louis Carré, Paris 1954, No. 54 repr., Musée Rath, Geneva 1955, No. 217, BN, Paris 1959, No. 121, Galerie Charpentier, Paris 1961, No. 184, Galerie Louis Carré, Paris 1963, No. 34, New Gallery Boom, Paris 1966.

Bibliography: A&P No. 334 repr.; cat. Hotel Drouot, Paris 1967,

Technique: Drypoint and engraving, two states.

Comment: This is a first state drypoint image, quite rare. A similar image was done the next year with the same techniques and title. This unsigned rare proof is from Raymond Haasen, son of Paul Haasen, Villon's printer. See page 278.

1941 "Jeune Femme"

Type:	Drypoint
Reference:	G&P: E455
Edition/Number:	First state--rare proof
Size--H, W:	11 x 8 inches
Framed:	Matted
Inventory Number:	JCL1146
Provenance:	W. F. Maibaum (8/14/1992)

Catherine

G&P: Burin (V.), 8.1 x 6.3 cm.
35 prints.

Exhibitions: Painters, Engravers, 1942, Musée Rath, Geneva 1955, No. 214, BN, Paris 1959, No. 119, Galerie Louis Carré, Paris 1963, No. 32; New Rise Gallery, Paris 1966.

Bibliography: A&P No. 332 repr. (Indicated by error: etching).

Technique: Basically a drypoint (burin) print.

Comment: I cannot discover the model for this work. It may have been done while Villon was in the South of France. He returned to Puteaux in 1942.

1941 "Catherine"

Type:	Dry Point (Burin)
Reference:	G&P: E452
Edition/Number:	35 /18
Size--H, W:	3-1/4 x 2 inches
Framed:	Matted
Inventory Number:	JCL2139
Provenance:	Annex Gallery #11615 (2/14/1994)

Portrait of Michel Mare, Architect

G&P: Lithograph in black, 33.2 x 23 cm signed and dated on the stone. 25 prints.

Exhibitions: "The Young Contemporary Engravers", London 1946; Gallery L. Goldschmidt, New York 1955, No. 39, Musée Rath, Geneva 1955, No. 260, BN, Paris 1959, No. 125, MDC, Le Havre, 1962, No. 76.

Bibliography: A&P No. 445 (dated erroneously 1943) repr.

Technique: Stone lithography.

Comment: Michel Mare was involved in reconstruction of Le Havre, was an illustrator for Andre Trannoy's book on Montalembert (1947) and is the parent of painter: Anne Laure Bayart Mare. Signed and dated on stone, pencil numbered, annotations, recto-pencil.

1942 "Portrait de Michel Mare, Architecte"

Type:	Lithograph
Reference:	G&P: E470
Edition/Number:	25 / 2
Size--H, W:	13-1/2 x 8 inches
Framed:	Yes
Inventory Number:	JCL0060
Provenance:	W. F. Maibaum/Walton-Gilbert: #6154

Young girl

G&P: Burin, 28.3 x 20.8 cm.
Some tests before trimming, 40 prints after trimming.

Exhibitions: Painters, Engravers, 1942; Prints modern French Ministry of Education, Montevideo 1947, No. 249; Museum of Modern Art, New York 1953, No. 79, Musée Rath, Geneva 1955, No. 216, Antwerp 1955, No. 205, B.N., Paris 1959, No. 120, repr. for the poster This Exhibition, Oslo 1958, No. 45, Galerie Louis Carré, Paris 1963, No. 35, Museum of Fine Arts, Boston 1964, No. 100 repr.

Bibliography: A&P. No. 335 repr.; cat. Hotel Drouot, Paris 1962, No. 88 repr., 1967, No. 69 repr.

1. MOMA, 1953, No. 79.
2. MFAB, 1964, No. 100, pictured page 62.
3. RSJ, 1976, No. 91, pictured page 53.

Technique: Pure drypoint engraving (burin). Pencil numbered, LL, signed, LR.

Comment: Stanley Johnson (1976) calls this an important work by Villon.

1942 "Jeune Fille"

Type:	Dry Point (Burin)
Reference:	G&P: E456
Edition/Number:	40 / 12
Size--H, W:	11 x 8 inches
Framed:	Matted
Inventory Number:	JCL0816
Provenance:	W. F. Maibaum (12/7/1991)

Celestial Globe, The Sky

G&P: Etching, 28 x 20.8 cm.
45 prints.
Etched directly from nature.

Exhibitions: Museum of Modern Art, New York 1953, No. 82; Gallery Louis Carré, Paris 1954, No. 57 repr. , Musée Rath, Geneva 1955, No. 222; Gallery L. Goldschmidt, New York 1955, No. 41, Antwerp 1955, No. 208 repr., Oslo 1958, No. 47; BN, Paris 1959, No. 128 repr.; Gallery Char-Carpentier, Paris 1961, No. 186, Museum of Fine Arts, Boston 1964, No. 103 repr.; Light Gallery, New York 1964, No. 84, New Rise Gallery, Paris 1966, Lisbon 1966, No. 18; Gallery G. Cramer, Geneva 1967, No. 36.

Bibliography: A&P. No. 347 repr.; cat. Hotel Drouot, Paris 1962, No. 73 repr.

1. MOMA, 1953, No. 88.
2. MFAB, 164, No. 103, pictured page 66.
3. L&S, 1964, No. 84.
4. AIC, 1976, No. 102.
5. FAM, 1976, No. 142, pictured, page 161.

Technique: Hard ground etching "directly from nature."

Comment: Susan Grace, of the Fogg museum, notes that the loose hatching shown in this image is typical of his later techniques. She also suggests that this etching is based upon earlier drawings and studies of similar-shaped objects, possibly an object he kept in his studio. There is also a painting dated 1925 with similar shapes and objects. Print obtained from Raymond Haasen, son of Paul Haasen, Villon's printer.

1944 "Globe Celeste, Le Ciel"

Type:	Etching
Reference:	G&P: $479
Edition/Number:	45 / unnumbered
Size--H, W:	11 x 8-1/8 inches
Framed:	Matted
Inventory Number:	JCL0733
Provenance:	W. F. Maibaum/Raymond Haasen, see comment opposite

Bird In A Cage or Composition

G&P: Etching and Burin
First state, 17.5 cm x 13 cm, ten artist proofs, thirty nine proofs altogether justified on one hand on fourteen and on the other on twenty five; final state, copper plate cut to the picture measurements (13.3 cm x 8.6 cm), new works, signature engraved (J.V.), Fifty proofs with wide margins and a printing to illustrate the book, *Les Mots Tracent*; published in Paris in 1951.

Bibliography: A&P. No. 381 repr.

Technique: Hard ground etching with drypoint.

Comment: The first state shows a faint outline of the "bird" and deep bites of the perspective lines. The plate and the lines were changed in hard ground etching to achieve the final state. The theoretical linear movement of the bird resulting in an all-at-one final state is consistent with Villon's approach.

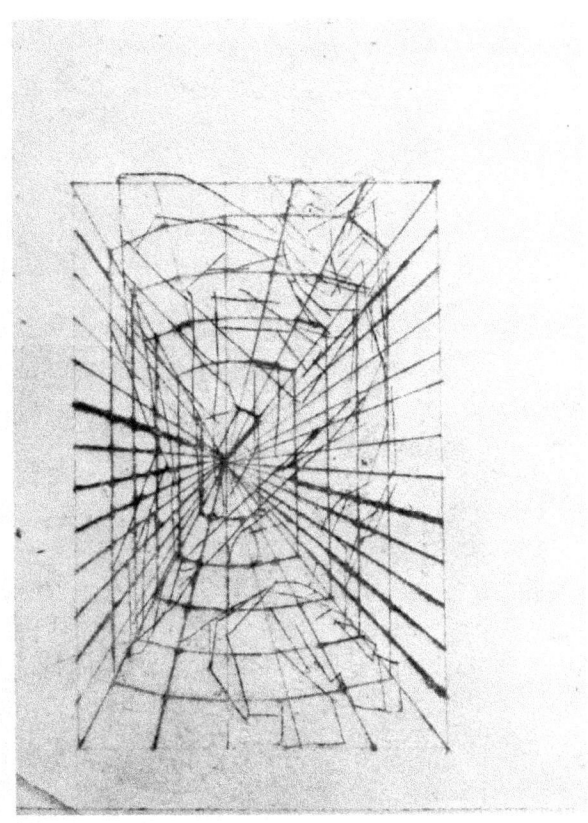

E 515.   1er état

1949 "Oiseau dans Cage"

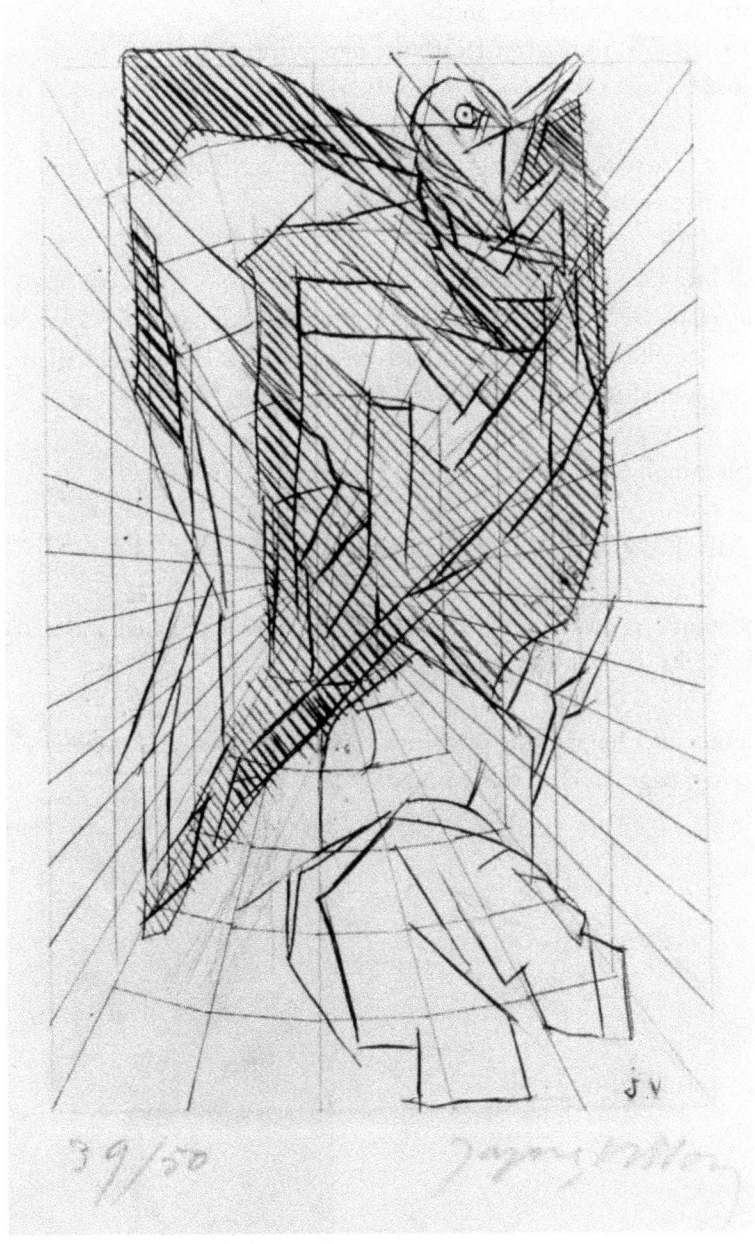

Type: Dry Point (Burin) and Etching
Reference: G&P: E515-final state
Edition/Number: 50 / 39
Size--H, W: 5-1/8 x 3 inches
Framed: Matted
Inventory Number: JCL1350
Provenance: Annex Gallery #EO102 (9/16/1992)

The Two Vases

Burin, signed and dated on the plate.
Forty proofs, printed in 1950, the new printing in 1955 to illustrate Jacques Lassaigne's book, Eulogy Of Jacques Villon, E 544 to 547. See Technique, below.

Note: There is a painting of the same subject, Towards Dream, 1947. As is Villon's method, the print is the reverse of the painting.

Exhibitions: Galerie Louis Carré, Paris 1954, No. 58; Rath Museum, Geneva 1955. No. 239, Antwerp 1955, No. 209, Galerie Louis Carré, Paris 1957, No. 36; Oslo 1958, No. 48; BN, Paris 1959, No. 138 repr.; French Institute, Athens 1958, Galerie Charpentier, Paris 1961, No. 187, Museum of Fine Arts, Boston 1964, No. 109 repr.

Bibliography: cat. Hotel Drouot, Paris 1962, No. 101.

1. MFAB, 1964, No. 109. Pictured page 71.

Technique: engraving/burin; essentially drypoint. Signed and dated on plate; pencil numbered LL ("19/30"), signed, LR.

Comment: The painting on which this work is based is shown below (from the Fogg museum catalog, page 163). It was painted in 1947.

1950 "Les Deux Vases"

Type:	Dry Point (Burin)
Reference:	G&P: E520
Edition/Number:	30 / 19 (In pencil on print, LL)
Size--H, W:	7-15/16 x 6 inches
Framed:	Yes
Inventory Number:	JCL0059
Provenance:	W. F. Maibaum F. A.

Lamps

G&P: Etching and aquatint, 24.5 x 27.3 cm.
First state without aquatint, a few trial proofs; second state, with aquatint, before signing, a few tests in black, 10 color prints on Japan and 10 artist's proofs, final state, color, signature and engraved date, 10 artist's proofs and 40 tests.

Exhibitions: Museum of Modern Art, New York 1953, 88 and 89 n...88 repr.; French Institute, Athens, 1958; Oslo in 1958, No. 51, NL, Paris 1959, No. 141, MDC, Le Havre 1962, No. 66, Museum of Fine Arts, Boston 1964, No. 110 repr.; Light Gallery, New York 1964, No. 101.

Bibliography: Cat. Hotel Drouot, Paris 1962 107, 1967, No. 98.

1. MOMA, 1953, No. 88 and 89, pictured page 23.
2. MMS, 1960.
3. MFAB, 1964, No. 110, pictured, page 71.
4. L&S, 1964, No. 101.

Technique: Hard ground etching with aquatint in color, three states.

Comment: A similar aquatint entitled "The Universe," was done in 1950 (and is pictured in color in the catalog of the Museum of Fine Arts, Boston, Color Plate No. 4. It is also the final print in the catalog of Cubist prints from the Philadelphia Museum of Art (No.29). In that print as in the present study, the objects are shown in cascading planes, in Villon's parlance, demonstrating the entire or "absolute" nature of the subject. This is a proof print of the second state. The first state was in hard ground etching only (below).

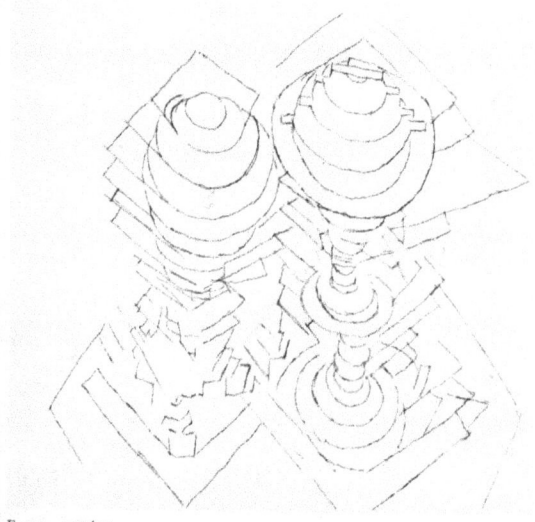

E 531. 1er état

1951 "Les Lampes"

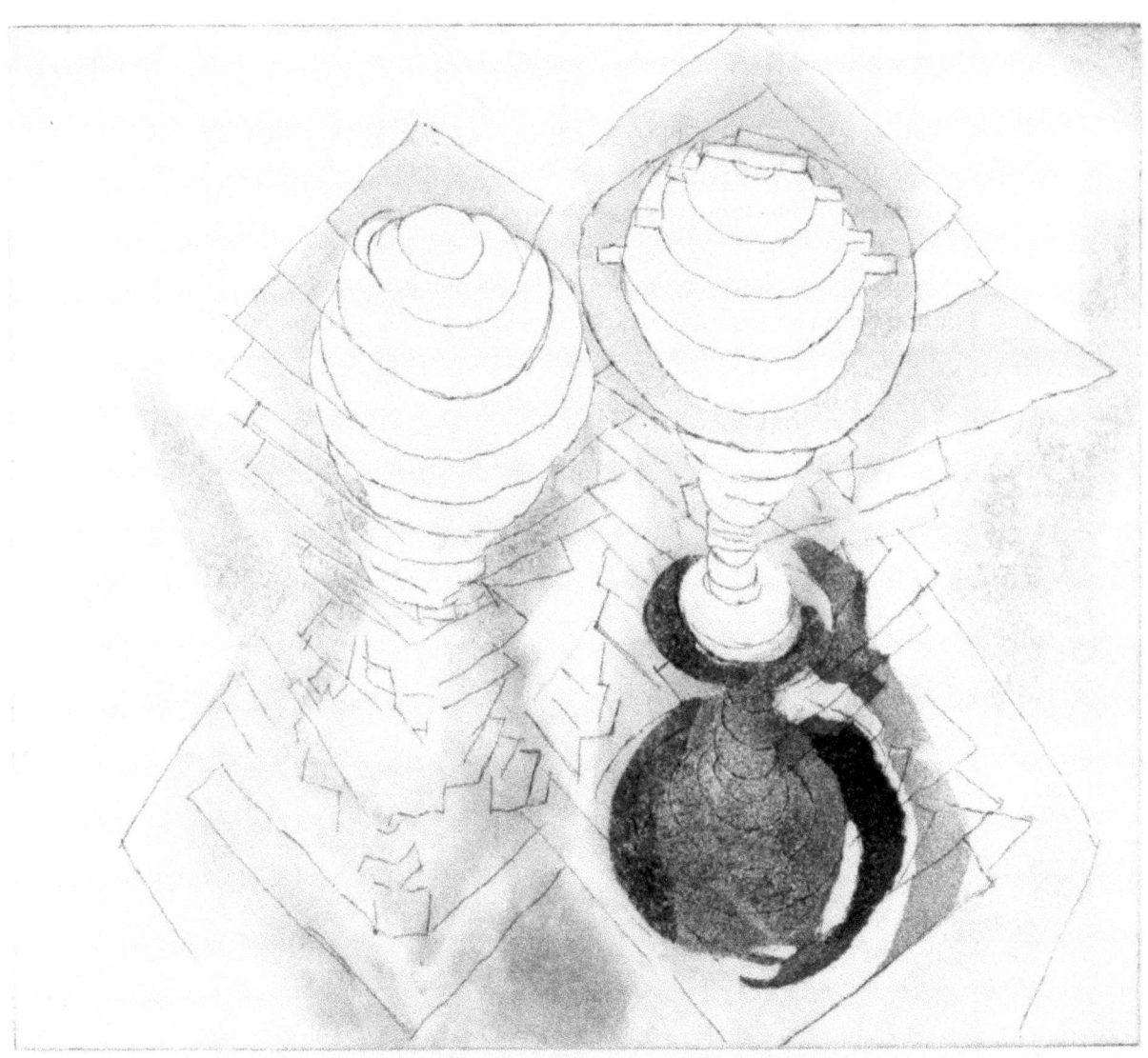

Type:	Etching and Aquatint (color)
Reference:	G&P: E531 ii/iii
Edition/Number:	10 / AP (Artist's Proof)
Size--H, W:	9-3/4 x 10 inches
Framed:	Yes
Inventory Number:	JCL2093
Provenance:	Steve Schmidt (San Francisco, CA) (12/29/1993)

Coursier I (Steed or Messenger)

G&P: Color lithograph, 46 x 29.5 cm.
220 prints and a few artist's proofs published by the Guild of Engraving .

Exhibition: M.D.C., Le Havre, 1962, No. 85.

Bibliography: Cat. Hotel Drouot, Paris 1962, No. 121.

Technique: Stone lithography in color, one state.

Comment: annotated on the reverse. Pencil numbered and signed. This is a lithograph prepared from a watercolor/gouache, shown on page 430, Leissring (2011).

1955 "Coursier I"

Type: Lithograph in color
Reference: G&P: App 101
Edition/Number: 220 / 101
Size--H, W: 11-5/8 x 18 inches
Framed: Matted
Inventory Number: JCL0774
Provenance: Published Guilde Gravure, Harcourts

The Two Vases

G&P: Engraving/Burin, 21 x 15.5 cm signed and dated on the plate.
40 prints made in 1950 and reissued in 1955 to illustrate the work of Jacques Lassaigne, In Praise of Jacques Villon, cf. E 544 to E 547

There is a painting of the same subject, Towards the Chimera, 1947.

Exhibitions: Galerie Louis Carré, Paris 1954, No. 58; Rath Museum, Geneva 1955. No. 239, Antwerp 1955, No. 209, Galerie Louis Carré, Paris 1957, No. 36; Oslo 1958, No. 48; BN, Paris 1959, No. 138 repr.; French Institute, Athens 1958, Galerie Charpentier, Paris 1961, No. 187, Museum of Fine Arts, Boston 1964, No. 109 repr.

Bibliography: Cat. Hotel Drouot, Paris 1962, No. 101.

1. MFAB, 1964, No. 109, Illustrated, page 71.

Technique: Engraving/burin, essentially drypoint.

Comment: See also page 95 for the earlier printed version of this important work. There is one additional print of this work, printed in 1955 in an edition of 200. The collection includes number 103 from that edition.

1955 "Les Deux Vases"

Type:	Dry Point (Burin)
Reference:	G&P: E520
Edition/Number:	30 / 13 (pencil numbered LL, signed LR)
Size--H, W:	8-1/8 x 6 inches
Framed:	Matted
Inventory Number:	JCL1433
Provenance:	W. F. Maibaum (11/16/1992)

The Bird

G&P: Etching, 10.1 x 16.8 cm signed and dated on the plate.

50 proofs in 1921, then reprinted in 1955 to illustrate the work of Jacques Lassaigne, Eloge de Jacques Villon, cf. E 544 to E 547.

Comment: Villon tastes in Cubism tend toward the discipline on which it was founded. This Cubism trapped the poetic universe to which he was bound not by strict images, but by its most fragile manifestation, the hopes and feelings of life.

Exhibitions: Musée Rath, Geneva 1955, No. 207, Galerie Louis Carré, Paris 1957, No. 7, French Institute, Athens 1958, BN, Paris 1959, No. 72, Galerie Charpentier, Paris 1961, No. 168, MDC, Le Havre 1962 No. 24, Light Gallery, New York 1964, No. 42 repr., Lisbon 1966, No. 8; Chicago 1967, No. 66 repr.; Museum of Fine Arts, Rouen, 1967; Gallery Sagot-Le Garrec, Paris 1975, No. 40 repr.

Bibliography: A&P No. 207 repr.; Graphis No. 53, repr.

1. L&S, 1964, No. 42, illustrated in catalog.
2. RSJ, 1967, No. 66, illustrated, page 47.

Technique: Hard ground etching, one state, reprinted in 1955.

Comment: This etching follows the one described on page 64, the Gallop or Horse. The use of planes to illustrate the motion of the bird (shown here) and the horse (page 65) suggests that he was working out his theoretical basis of his Cubist/Section d'Or philosophy. This philosophy is discussed in the essay.

Villon chose to include this plate in the Lassaigne book, Eulogy of Jacques Villon (1928/1955).

1955 "Oiseau"

Type:	Etching plate signed and dated 1921
Reference:	G&P: E293
Edition/Number:	200 / 103
Size--H, W:	4-1/16 x 6 inches
Framed:	Matted
Inventory Number:	JCL1734
Provenance:	W. F. Maibaum (1/19/1993)

The Table With a Black Stamp

G&P: Dry Point Etching
First state, dry point, a few proofs; second state, reworked with etching, signature and date engraved, a few proofs; final state, with new works after the trimming of the copper plate, fifty proofs. New printing in 1955, to illustrate Jacques Lassaign's book, Eulogy of Jacques Villon. Cf. E544-547. Subject from a 1925 painting.

Exhibitions: Galerie Louis Carré, Paris 1957, No. 18, French Institute, Athens 1958, BN, Paris 1959, No. 86 (3 states); Stockholm 1960 No. 118, Light Gallery, New York 1964, Nos. 58 and 59.

Bibliography: A&P. 235 repr.; cat. Hotel Drouot, Paris 1962, No. 34.

1. MMS, 1960, No. 118.
2. L&S, 1954, Nos. 58, 59.

Technique: Drypoint with hard ground etching, two states, second state below.

Comment: This is another image chosen to illustrate the Lassaigne book: Eulogy of Jacques Villon.

E 348. 2e état

1955 "La Table Au Tampon Noir"

Type:	Dry Point and Etching plated signed and dated "26"
Reference:	G&P: E348
Edition/Number:	200 / 103
Size--H, W:	5-3/8 x 4 inches
Framed:	Matted
Inventory Number:	JCL1735
Provenance:	W. F. Maibaum (1/19/1993)

Coursier I (Study)

Unique watercolor/gouache. a study for "Coursier I" described in G&P as follows:

Coursier I
Color lithograph, 46 x 29.5 cm.
220 trials and a few artist's proofs published by the Guild of Engraving.

Exhibition: M.D.C., Le Havre, 1962, No. 85.

Bibliography: Cat. Hotel Drouot, Paris 1962, No. 121.

Technique: Watercolor and gouache on paper.

Comment: A unique study in preparation for the lithograph, also done in 1955 and shown on pages 98-99.

1955 "Coursier I, study"

Type:	Painting: Gouache/watercolor
Reference:	Unique study for lithograph on page 99
Edition/Number:	Unique
Size--H, W:	11-3/4 x 18 inches
Framed:	Yes
Inventory Number:	JCL3437
Provenance:	Harcourt's Gallery, San Francisco, CA

Bird in Flight

G&P: Lithograph, 5 colors, 46 x 26.5 cm.
220 prints and artist proofs published by the Guild of Engraving.

Exhibition: M.D.C., Le Havre 1962, No. 83.

Technique: Stone lithography in five colors.

Comment: Villon returns to some of his earlier ideas. In 1921, he did Le Cheval (page 65) and two years earlier than this work, he painted a study for Coursier I (page 107) and completed a lithograph of Coursier I (page 99).

1957 "Oiseau en Vol"

109

Type: Lithograph in color
Reference: G&P: App 99
Edition/Number: 220 / 10
Size--H, W: 10-1/2 x 18 inches
Framed: Matted
Inventory Number: JCL2143
Provenance: Annex Gallery, # Pink101 (2/14/1994)

Anger

G&P: Etching, 18.8 x 13 cm.
From "Poetic Works" text by Robert Ganzo,
8 illustrative etchings as inserts, including 2 in color, with colophon:
"There were printed for this work, 10 copies on ancient Japan paper, including an original drawing, a copper plate, a suite in the first state a suite in sanguine; 25 copies on Arches paper, numbered from 11 to 35, including the frontispiece in the first state a suite in sanguine, 150 copies on vellum *pur fil Marais*, numbered from 36 to 185."

All copies are signed by the poet and the artist. The etchings were graven in collaboration with Fiorini, and printed on presses G. Leblanc, Paris, Marcel Sauticr, publisher, Paris 1957.

Technique: Hard ground etching, No. 152 of a run of 185. Signed on colophon.

Comment: A beautiful etching of a symbolic form of anger. There are three other etchings of this work in the collection ranging from proofs through the suite in sanguine above.

Robert Ganzo, amateur archaeologist, became interested in prehistory and was in 1958, the discoverer of the major prehistoric sites, in Villeneuve-sur-Auvers and D'Huisson-Longueville (Essonne).

1957 "La Colere"

Type:	Etching
Reference:	G&P: App 17
Edition/Number:	10 / 4
Size--H, W:	7-1/8/ x 5 inches
Framed:	No
Inventory Number:	JCL2457, JCL2439, JCL2448, JCL2643
Provenance:	W. F. Maibaum F. A., Annex Gallery

Effort

Watercolor with gouache on paper. Unique. A study for the graphic also entitled "Effort," three states of which are shown below. The work, as a graphic, accompanied a poem by Andrew Frénaud, Effort. It was in dry point with etching. As is the usual method with Villon, the graphic is the reverse of the painting, for it was used as the guide for the drawing upon the plate; the prints are thus "reversed."

The image is shown on the cover in color.

E 553. 1ᵉʳ état

E 586. 2ᵉ état

E 586. Etat définitif

1958 L'Effort"

113

Type: Watercolor with gouache on paper
Reference: Study for G&P: E586
Edition/Number: Unique
Size--H, W: 19-3/4 x 12 inches
Framed: Yes
Inventory Number: JCL3340
Provenance: Steve Schmidt, San Francisco, CA (Verification letter)

Maiden or Young Girl

G&P: Lithograph in black, 53.5 x 40 cm.

Exhibition poster Jacques Villon in the National Library, Paris 1959
Indeterminate number of tests before the signature.

Mourlot printer.

Lithographic version of an etching of 1942 (E. 456). Page 89, Pencil signed LR.

Technique: Stone lithography in black. This print is for a poster (1959) announcing an exhibition of Villon's works in the National Library of Paris. The image is based upon the 1942 etching discussed on page 89. The etching size is 11" X 8" and is shown below.

E 456.

1959 "Jeune Fille"

Type:	Lithograph in black
Reference:	G&P: App III
Edition/Number:	Proof
Size--H, W:	21-1/4 x 16 inches
Framed:	Matted
Inventory Number:	JCL1148
Provenance:	W. F. Maibaum F. A. (8/14/1991)

Equilibrist

Lithograph in Color, annotated Artist's Proof, signed, rare.

Technique: Stone lithography in color. Artist's proof, signed.

Comment: Villon, now at age 80, returns to an earlier idea that he has used several times in other forms and techniques. In 1914, for example, "Le Petite Equilibriste," pages 51, 53, and 55.

1960 "Equilibriste"

117

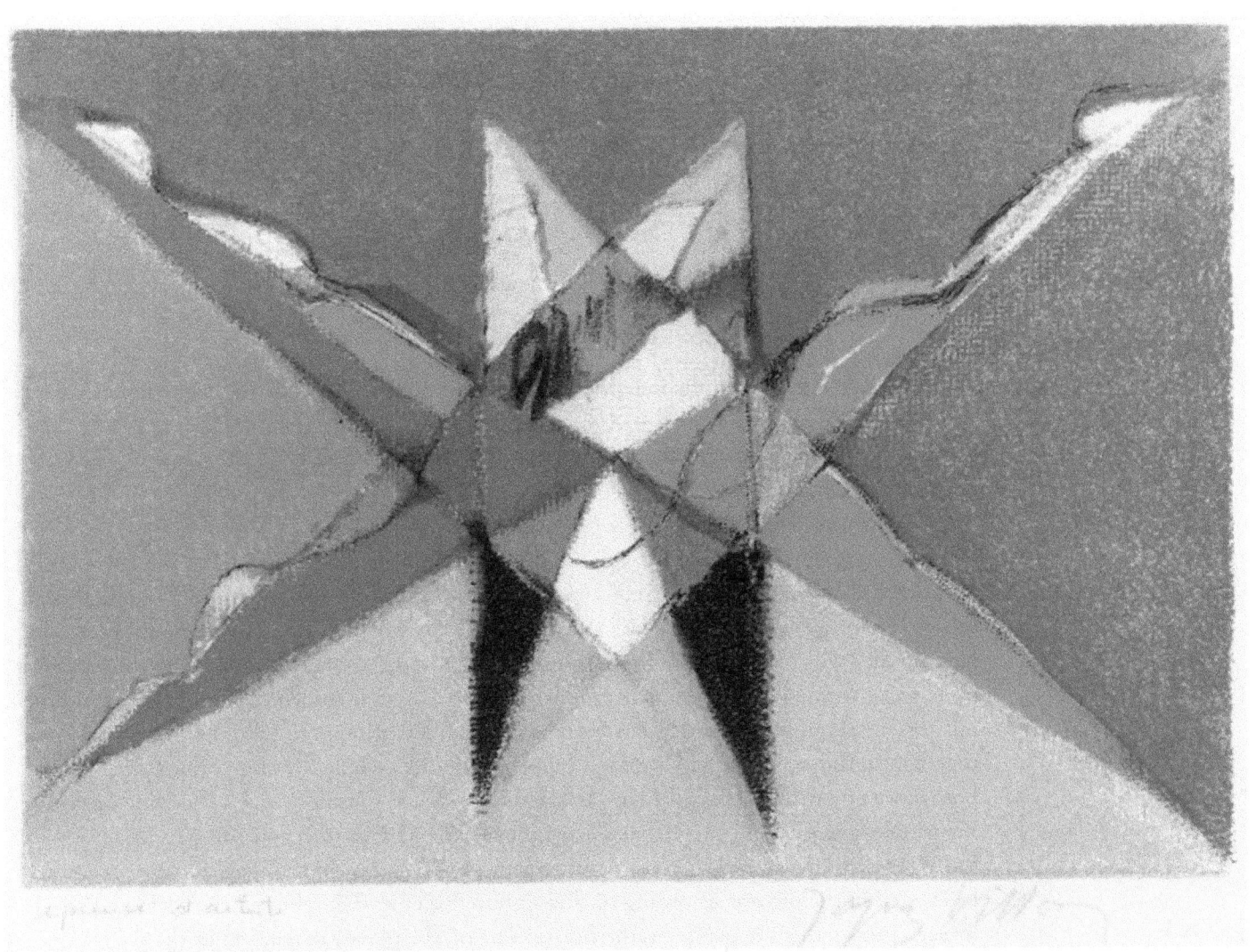

Type: Lithograph in color
Reference: Annotated artist's proof (not in G&P)
Edition/Number: Proof
Size--H, W: 6-5/16 x 8 inches
Framed: Matted
Inventory Number: JCL0694
Provenance: Annex Gallery (12/8/1990)

Jacques Villon; Presented by Lionello Venturi

G&P: Book size 43 x 53 cm, in Italian, bound in beige cloth illustrated with 8 original lithographs in color by Jacques Villon, in full page, all signed by the artist.

The edition was limited to 225 numbered copies of which there are 25 copies on Japan imperial nacre, 175 copies on Arches; 25 copies marked "not for sale" on Arches. An additional two suites of lithographs on Japan imperial nacre and 25 suites on Arches. were published." Mourlot, printer, Louis Carré, publisher, Paris 1962.

Papers
Color lithograph.
Drawing as described above.
Reproduction of a painting from 1932.

Technique: Stone lithography in color. Ed. of 175, No. 152. On Arches. Signed, pencil LR.

Comment: This is an image taken from a painting in oil referred to in the following narrative between Dora Vallier and Villon:

"Not only are the colours from the tubes different from the colours of light, but there is also a world of difference in the way colours from the tube and those of light link among themselves. For instance, once I have laid the very first tone, which is taken from the local one, I have no idea which colours are going to follow. It's not up to me to choose. The chromatic circle is going to show them to me, because the chromatic circle on which hues of light and their nuances are set in perfect order, has been so calculated that one can tell how these hues link together. In this way, when I have found on the chromatic circle the two colours that go on both sides of my first tone, all I have to do is to go all over again through the same operation. First I take one of these two colours, then the other and each one, according to its position in the chromatic circle, brings two new colours on to the canvas. In this way, all colours come to be located in the picture according to their interferences in the light and the surface covered by each one of them depends on the positioning of the planes in relation to the source of light. There are always different planes — don't you think so? There is one that comes forward followed by another one while a third remains further back. On the canvas they overlap, but their intersections are always there and they reveal the planes and assign to each colour its precise place.

1962 "Papiers"

Type:	Lithograph in color
Reference:	G&P: App 65
Edition/Number:	175 / 152
Size--H, W:	11-3/4 x 14 inches
Framed:	Yes
Inventory Number:	JCL0099
Provenance:	W. F. Maibaum F. A. (1/14/1988)

To The Chimera (Daydream Verse)

G&P: Color lithograph.
Drawing as described above, Page 118.
Reproduction of a painting from 1942.

Technique: Stone lithography in color, Ed. of 175, No. 152; on Rives. Signed, pencil, LR.

Comment: this is another lithographic version of a favorite painting from 1942.

1962 "Vers la Chimere"

Type:	Lithograph in color
Reference:	G&P: App 68
Edition/Number:	175 / 152
Size--H, W:	14-1/8 x 11 inches
Framed:	Yes
Inventory Number:	JCL0102
Provenance:	W. F. Maibaum F. A. (1/14/1988)

Harlequin

Not in G&P; Lithograph in color; artist's proof.

Technique: Stone lithography in color, artist's proof.

Comment: The work is plate signed and dated: "Villon 1914"; plate signed/dated "H Deschamps Lith 1962";, pencil "Epreuve d'Artiste", pencil signed by the artist lower right. The commentary suggests this is after a 1914 work, possibly a painting from 1914.

1962 "Arlequin"

Type:	Lithograph in color
Reference:	Not in G&P
Edition/Number:	Proof
Size--H, W:	23 x 11 inches
Framed:	Matted
Inventory Number:	JCL0696
Provenance:	Annex Gallery #10617 (12/8/1990)

Prometheus Unbound

G&P: Lithograph in black, 40 x 30 cm.
Print run unspecified. This is a very rare proof (in black).
Reproduction of a painting, study for the decoration of the Technical School de Cachan.

Technique: Stone lithography in color, very small edition, proof reproduction in aquatint. Signed and annotated in pencil, LL, LR.

Comment: The much esteemed and famous printer, Raymond Haasen worked with Villon in creating this and similar lithographs (see Pages: 270, 318, 320, 622, 626, Leissring, 2011). The work is plate signed lower right and pencil initialled "HC", lower right. Drawn on stone by Haasen, hand-colored & stencilled by Villon; portfolio never published; very few proofs. Signed in pencil by Villon, lower left. In his book, "About Prints," Stanley Hayter described the work-shop of Raymond Haasen, as follows:

"Near the Place d'Italie there is to be found another of these workshops, that of Raymond Haasen, still bearing the name of Paul Haasen, his father, who printed my 'Paysages Urbains' for me in 1930. Most of the intaglio prints of Chagall are still made and printed in this workshop. Here in the small atelier of the patron himself is a great press; on different floors of the building a press-room with eight more presses—now, alas, mostly idle—and a complete and very modern workshop where serigraphy, mechanized to some extent, is carried on. Raymond Haasen may well be the most competent master printer in Paris: his descent from Paul Haasen, once contre-maitre of the atelier of Paul Delatre who printed the Meryon plates at the beginning of the century, and his long and varied experience of the craft could lead one to expect it. An artist in his own right, the only student, with Jacques Villon, of the art of interpretative colour aquatint in those years when he was making the colour reproductions for Braun already referred to, at twenty-two he was already a master printer and (echo of the ancient guilds) obtained for four colour prints etched and printed by his own hand the diploma of 'Meilleur Ouvrier de France'. Does anyone, I wonder, still labour for such honour, and are there people left to respect, or even to judge, the competitors for such a distinction? His real titles to distinction are the reproductions made by most unorthodox methods in collaboration with Fernand Leger and applications of orthodox plate methods in incredible reproductions; and even some prints of plates of mine which I had entirely forgotten."

1962 "Promethee Delivre"

Type:	Lithograph in black
Reference:	G&P: App119
Edition/Number:	Very small--this is a proof
Size--H, W:	15-1/8 x 11 inches
Framed:	Yes
Inventory Number:	JCL2134 (also 1149, 2085, 2089, 2090 [color])
Provenance:	L. Saphire/W. F. Maibaum F. A. (2/23/1994)

Sources

1. Jacques Villon, Master of Graphic Art, Museum of Fine Arts, Boston, MA, 1964, Library of Congress Card No. 64-17722.

2. Jacques Villon, 1875-1963, The Art Institute of Chicago, 1976, Library of Congress Card No. 76-24972.

3. Jacques Villon, Daniel Robbins, Ed., Fogg Art Museum, Harvard University, Cambridge, MA, 1976, ISBN 0-916724-01-8.

4. Jacques Villon and his Cubist Prints, Innis Howe Shoemaker, Philadelphia Museum of Art, 2001, ISBN 0-87633-153-3.

5. A Collection of Graphic Work, 1896-1913, in Rare or Unique Impressions by Jacques Villon, Lucien Goldschmidt, Inc, New York, NY, 1970.

6. Master of Graphic Art, Jacques Villon, 1875-1963, R. S. Johnson International Galleries, Chicago, Il, 1967.

7. Jacques Villon, 1875-1963, A Selection of Rare Etchings, Aquatints and Drypoints acquired mainly from the collection of the late Louis Carré, R. S. Johnson International, 1978.

8. Jacques Villon, his Graphic Art, The Museum of Modern Art Bulletin, Vol. XXI, No.1, Fall, 1953.

9. Homage to Jacques Villon, 1875-1963, A Retrospective of the First thirty years of the Artist's Graphic Work, 1891-1921, Winter, 1975-76, R. S. Johnson International, Chicago, Il.

10. Unpacking Duchamp, Art in Transit, Judovitz, Dalia, U. Calif. Press, Berkeley, 1995, ISBN 0-520-08809-3.

11. The World of Marcel Duchamp, 1887, Tomkins, Calvin, Time-Life Books, 1966, LCC 66-28544

12. Marcel Duchamp, The Box in a Valise, Bonk, Ecke, David Britt, trans., Rizzoli International Publication, 1989, ISBN 0-8478-0979-X.

13. Marcel Duchamp, D'Harnoncourt, Anne, McShine, Kynaston, Eds., Museum of Modern Art, 1989, ISBN 3-7913-1018-6.

14. Duchamp, Faerna, Jose Maria, ed., Great Modern Masters, Harry Abrams, 1995/6, ISBN 0-8109-4678-5.

15. The Brothers Duchamp, Exhibition Catalog, Arnold Herstand and Co., NY, 1986.

16. Les 3 Duchamp, Cahanne, Pierre (text), Editions Ides et Calendes, 1975.

16a. The Brothers Duchamp, Cahanne, Pierre, text, Translated by Delga and Dinah Harrison, New York Graphic Society, Boston, 1976. ISBN: 0-8212-0666-4.

17. Marcel Duchamp, Work and Life, Gough-Cooper, Jennifer and Caummont, Jacques, text, MIT Press, Cambridge, MA, 1993. ISBN 0-262-08225-Xr.

18. Marcel Duchamp, Sarane Alexandrian, Bonfini Press Corp., Naefels, Switzerland, 1977, ISBN 0-517-53008-2r.

19. Marcel Duchamp, Appearance Stripped Bare, Octavio Paz, Seaver books, 1978, Arcade Publishing, NY, 1990, ISBN 1-55970-138-2r.

20. The Definitively Unfinished Marcel Duchamp, Thierry de Duve, Ed., MIT Press, Cambridge, MA, 1991, ISBN 0-262-04117-0.

21. Marcel Duchamp, Gloria Moure, Rizzoli International Publications, MY, 1988, ISBN 0-8478-0978-1.

22. Jacques Villon, 1875-1963, a Retrospective Exhibition, Neuberger Museum, SUNY, Purchase, NY, 1976, Text by Francis Steegmuller.

23. Duchamp, A Biography, Tomkins, Calvin, Holt and Co., New York, 1996. ISBN: 0-8050-0823-3.

24. The Complete Printmaker, Techniques, Traditions, Innovations, Ross, John, Romano, Clare, Ross, Tim, The Free Press, Division, Collier Macmillan, Publishers, New York, London, 1990, ISBN: 0-02-927371-4.

25. On Growth and Form, D'Arcy Thompson, Cambridge University Press, 1961, 2010, ISBN: 978-0-521-43776-9.

26. The Golden Ratio, The Story of Phi, the World's most Astonishing Number, Mario Livio, Random House, 2002, ISBN: 0-7679-0815-5.

27. Modern Chromatics, Ogden N. Rood, Van Nostrand Reinhold Co., New York, 1879, 1973. ISBN:0-442-27028-3.

28. Selected Writings of Paul Valéry, New Directions Publishing Corp., New York, 1964, ISBN: 978-0-8112-0213-8.

29. The Geometry of Art and Life, Ghyka, Matila, Dover Publications, 1977. ISBN: 0-486-23542-4.

30. A Treatise on Painting, da Vinci, Leonardo, John F. Rigaud, Translation, Dover Publications, 2005, ISBN: 0-486-44155-5.

31 Memoirs of a Dada Drummer, Richard Huelsenbeck, Hans Kleinschmidt, Ed. University of California Press, Berkeley, 1991, ISBN: 0-20-07370-3.

32. Modern Chromatics, Ogden N. Rood, Van Nostrand Reinhold Co., New York, 1879, 1973. ISBN:0-442-27028-3.

33. Tristes Tropiques, Lévi-Strauss, Claude, Translated by John and Doreen Weightman, Penguin Books, 1992. ISBN: 978-0-14-016562-3.

34. The Elements of Color, Johannes Itten, Ernst Van Hagen, Translator, John Wiley and Sons, Inc. New York, 2001, ISBN: 0-471-28929-9.

35. Poems, Francois Villon, Peter Dale, Translator, Anvil Press Poetry, 2001, ISBN:978-0-85646-323-5.

36. Collected Poems and Other Verse, Stéphane Mallarmé, E. H. and A. M. Blackmore, Translators, Oxford University Press, 2008, ISBN: 978-0-19-953792-1.

37. About Prints, Hayter, S. W., Oxford University press, London, 1962, Gallery, Inc. 1964.

38. Jacques Villon, Master Printmaker, Exhibition Catalog, R. M. Light and Co., Helene C. Seiferheld Gallery, Inc., New York, 1964. "Jacques Villon, An Appreciation," Francis Steegmuller.

Abbreviations and Referenced Catalogs

1. A&P, 1950 Jacques Villon, Catalog of his Engraved Work, Auberty and Perussaux, Paris, 1950.

2. MOMA, 1953 Jacques Villon, his Graphic Work, Bulletin, Vol. XXL, No. 1. Museum of Modern Art, New York, 1953.

3. SRGM, 1957 Jacques Villon, Raymond Duchamp-Villon, Marcel Duchamp, 1957, Solomon R. Guggenheim Museum, NY.

4. B-N, 1959 Jacques Villon, Engraved Work, Bibliotheque Nationale, Paris, 1959.

5. MMS, 1960 Moderna Museet Stockholm, March, 1960.

6. EVT, 1964 Jacques Villon, Paintings, 1909-1960, March-April, 1964, E. V. Thaw and Co., New York.

7. L&S, 1964 Jacques Villon, Master Printmaker, Light and Seiferheld, Helene Seiferheld Gallery, Inc., New York, 1964.

8. MFAB, 1964 Jacques Villon, Master of Graphic Art, Museum of Fine Arts, Boston, 1964.

9. RSJ, 1967 Jacques Villon, Master of Graphic Art, R. S. Johnson International, Chicago, 1967.

10. LGI, 1970 Jacques Villon, A Collection of Graphic Work, 1896-1913, in rare or unique impressions, Lucien Goldschmidt, incorporated, 1970.

11. RSJ, 1974 19th and 20th Century Master Graphics, .R. S. Johnson Fine Art, 1974.

12. RSJ, 1975 Homage to Jacques Villon, R. S. Johnson International, Chicago, 1975.

13. AIC, 1976 Jacques Villon, Art Institute of Chicago, 1976.

14. FAM, 1976 Jacques Villon, Robbins, Daniel, Ed.
Fogg Art Museum, 1976.

15. RSJ, 1976 Important 19th and 20th Century Master Graphics, R. S. Johnson Fine Art, 1976.

16. RSJ, 1978 Jacques Villon, Works from the Collection of the late Louis Carré, R. S. Johnson International, Chicago, 1978.

17. G&P, 1979 Villon, Prints and Illustrations, Catalogue Raisonné, Ginestet and Pouillon, Jacques, 1979.

18. LGI, 1979 Jacques Villon, Sixty Drawings and Watercolors, 1894-1954, Lucien Goldschmidt, Inc. N.Y., 1979.

19. RSJ, 1980 Twentieth Century Master Graphics, Matisse, Picasso, Villon, Vlaminck, R. S. Johnson Fine Art, 1980.

20. RSJ, 1983 Important 19th and 20th century Master Graphics, R. S. Johnson Fine Art, 1983.

21. RMA, 1984 Jacques Villon, Graphic Work, Rijks Museum, Amsterdam, 1984.

22. RSJ, 1988 European Prints and drawings, 1890-1980, R. S. Johnson Fine Art, 1988.

23. RSJ, 1989A American and European Master Graphics, 1890-1980, R. S. Johnson Fine Art, 1989.

24. RSJ, 1989B Cubism and La Section d'Or, Works on paper, 1907-1922, R. S. Johnson Fine Art, 1989.

25. RSJ, 1990 A. L De Sanctis Collection, Works on Paper: Manet to Picasso, R. S. Johnson Fine Art, 1990.

26. RSJ, 1991 Cubism and La Section D'Or, R. S. Johnson Fine Art, 1991.

27. DIA, 1995 Jacques Villon, Printmaker, Detroit Institute of Arts, 1995.

28. RSJ, 1999A Renoir to George Grosz, Paintings, Works on Paper, R. S. Johnson Fine Art, 1999.

29. RSJ, 1999B Degas to Magritte, Paintings, Sculpture, Works on Paper, R. S. Johnson Fine Art, 1999.

30. PMA, 2001 Jacques Villon and His Cubist Prints, Philadelphia Museum of Art, 2001.

31. RSJ, 2001 Aspects of Art in France, Renoir to Gleizes, R. S. Johnson Fine Art, 2001.

32. RSJ, 2003 Works on Paper, 1875-1975, R. S. Johnson Fine Art, 2003.

33. RSJ, 2005 Master Graphics, R. S. Johnson Fine Art, 2005.

34. RSJ, 2006 Paintings, works on paper, sculpture, 1880-1970, R. S. Johnson Fine Art, 2006.

For complete information and cross-references to all of the Villon work on paper in the collection of J. C. Leissring Fine Art, please consult:
Jacques Villon
Jacques Villon in the Collection of Jack Leissring
ISBN: 978-0-9630085-1-0
J. C. Leissring Fine Art Press
Santa Rosa, CA

Colophon:
Designed and type-set in Adobe InDesign©. Photography by Ron Chamberlain and J. Leissring. Digital conversions in Corel Photo Impact X3©. Final proof reading by Julie Anne Tomlinson, curator of J. C. Leissring Fine Art.

133